Microsoft®

OFFICE^{XP}

New Features
GUIDE

Changes from
Office 2000 to Office XP

**COURSE
TECHNOLOGY**

™

THOMSON LEARNING

Australia • Canada • Mexico • Singapore
Spain • United Kingdom • United States

VP and GM of Courseware:	Michael Springer
Series Product Managers:	Caryl Bahner-Guhin, Charles G. Blum, and Adam A. Wilcox
Developmental Editor:	Josh Pincus
Production Editor:	Karen Jacot
Project Editor:	Debbie Masi
Key Tester:	Bill Bateman
Series Designer:	Adam A. Wilcox
Cover Designer:	Steve Deschene

For more information contact:

Course Technology
25 Thomson Place
Boston, MA 02210

Or find us on the Web at: www.course.com

For permission to use material from this text or product, contact us by

- Web: www.thomsonrights.com
- Phone: 1-800-730-2214
- Fax: 1-800-730-2215

Trademarks

Course ILT is a trademark of Course Technology.

Some of the product names and company names used in this book have been used for identification purposes only and may be trademarks or registered trademarks of their respective manufacturers and sellers.

Disclaimer

Course Technology reserves the right to revise this publication and make changes from time to time in its content without notice.

ISBN 0-619-10968-8

Printed in the United States of America

1 2 3 4 5 BH 04 03 02 01

Contents

Unit 1

Task panes, smart tags, and the Ask a Question box

Unit time: 50 minutes

Complete this unit, and you'll know how to:

A Open and close task panes, and use them to create new Office files, open existing files, and search for files.

B Work with smart tags.

C Access Help by using the Ask a Question box.

Topic A: Introducing task panes

Explanation   Office XP comes with several new features and improvements over Office 2000. One of them is task panes, which provide a convenient interface through which you can perform common tasks.

Task pane basics

With the exception of Outlook, all Office XP programs have an integrated task pane that appears on the right side of the program window. These *task panes* provide a convenient interface through which users can perform common tasks. For example, you can use Word's task pane to open a recently used document, create a new document, send an e-mail, perform file searches, or access Help. If the task pane is closed, it appears automatically when you initiate an action that requires its use—for example, when you choose File, New to create a new workbook in Excel.

Each task pane is actually a series of task panes, some of which are shared across multiple Office programs. Word, PowerPoint, and Excel have four task panes in common: Clipboard, Basic Search, Advanced Search, and Insert Clip Art. Access has three of these (it lacks Insert Clip Art). Each Office program also has its own "New" task pane. For example, Excel has a New Workbook task pane, and Word has a New Document task pane. These "New" task panes are basically the same in form and function, but are tailored to the particular needs of the parent program.

In addition, PowerPoint and Word both provide a series of unique, program-specific task panes. These include the Mail Merge task pane of Word and the Slide Layout task pane of PowerPoint.

Showing and hiding task panes

The task pane is displayed by default in Word, PowerPoint, Excel, and Access. If you want the task pane to remain hidden when you start a particular Office program, clear the Show at startup option (at the bottom of the task pane). Of course, you can also check this option if you want the task pane to automatically appear when you start the program. Either way, please note that this setting applies to only the current program.

If the task pane is closed, you can open it by choosing View, Task Pane, or by initiating an action for which it's required (for example, creating a new workbook).

Exhibit 1-1: The New Presentation task pane

Do it!

A-1:   Examining task panes

Here's how	Here's why
1 Start Word	Note that the New Document task pane appears by default on the right side of the window.
2 Click as shown	To display the task pane menu.
Observe the menu	It's divided into two sections. The top four task panes are shared across Word, PowerPoint, Excel, and Access. The bottom four task panes are available in only Word.
Click anywhere outside the menu	To close it.
3 Clear **Show at startup**	(At the bottom of the task pane.) With this option cleared, the task pane will not automatically appear when you start Word.

4 Close Word

5 Start PowerPoint

Note that the task pane appears automatically, as shown in Exhibit 1-1. This demonstrates that if you clear "Show at startup" in one Office program, the new setting doesn't carry over to any other program. Also, notice that the default task pane is New Presentation. This task pane serves the same purpose as the New Document task pane in Word, but it's tailored to PowerPoint.

Display the task pane menu

✓	New Presentation
	Clipboard
	Search
	Insert Clip Art
	Slide Layout
	Slide Design - Design Templates
	Slide Design - Color Schemes
	Slide Design - Animation Schemes
	Custom Animation
	Slide Transition

Again, the task panes in the top section are shared across most of the Office suite, while those in the bottom section are unique to PowerPoint.

Close the task pane menu

Click anywhere outside of it.

6 Clear **Show at startup**

7 Close PowerPoint

8 Start Word

Because you cleared the Show at startup option, the task pane remains hidden until you open it manually, or until you initiate an action for which it's required.

Choose **File, New...**

To display the New Document task pane, which you can use to create a new document.

9 Close Word

Creating Office files

Explanation

You can use the "New" task pane to create blank Office files or files based on existing files. For example, in Word, you can create a new document by clicking Blank Document in the New Document task pane.

To create a new Word document based on an existing one:

1 Under New from existing document, click Choose Document to open the New from Existing Document dialog box.

2 Navigate to the folder that contains the desired document.

3 Select the document, and then click Create New to create a copy of the selected document. To prevent you from overwriting the original document, the new document is given a generic name (Document#) by default. You should give the file a meaningful name when you save it.

You can use basically the same procedures in PowerPoint, Excel, and Access.

Do it!

A-2:   Creating new Office files

Here's how	Here's why
1 Start PowerPoint	You'll create a blank presentation.
2 Display the New Presentation task pane	Choose File, New or choose View, Task Pane.
Under New, observe the available options	**New** ☐ Blank Presentation ☐ From Design Template ☐ From AutoContent Wizard
	By using the New Presentation task pane, you can create a blank presentation or a template based presentation. You can also use the AutoContent Wizard to create a presentation containing sample text in each slide.
3 Under New, click **Blank Presentation**	To create a new, blank presentation. Notice that the task pane changes to Slide Layout.
4 Under Apply slide layout, select any layout	(From the Text Layouts or Content Layouts list.) The selected layout is applied to the first slide.
Explore some other layouts	(Click them.) This demonstrates that you can use the task pane to apply a different slide layout with a single click.
5 Close PowerPoint	Don't save the presentation.

6	Start Word	You'll create a new document based on an existing one. In other words, you'll make a copy of an existing document and save it under a new name.
	Display the New Document task pane	
7	Under New from existing document, click **Choose document**	To open the New from Existing Document dialog box.
8	Navigate to **C:\Student Data**	You'll see a list of unit folders for this course.
	Double-click the current unit folder	To display its contents.
9	Select **About OS**	If necessary.
	Click **Create New**	To create a copy of the existing document.
10	Observe the title bar	"Document2 – Microsoft Word" appears on the title bar indicating that it's a new file containing the contents of the original file. You'll need to save it with another name.
11	Save the document as **My about OS**	In the current unit folder.
	Close the document	
12	Close Word	

Opening Office files

Explanation

You can open Office files by using the File menu or the "New" task pane. The last four recently used files appear as links under the "Open" option in the "New" task pane. For example, in the New Workbook task pane, you can click a file name from the list under Open a workbook to open the recently used workbook. Note that this list of files that appears in the task pane is the same as the recently used file list in the File menu.

Do it!

A-3: Opening existing Office files

Here's how	Here's why
1 Start Excel	You'll open a workbook by using the New Workbook task pane.
2 Under Open a workbook, click **Workbooks...**	To display the Open dialog box.
3 Navigate to the current unit folder	
4 Select **Sales figures**	If necessary.
Click **Open**	
5 Close Excel	
6 Start Word	
7 Display the New Document task pane	
Observe the recently used file list	**Open a document** My about OS 🗁 More documents...
	The file, "My about OS" appears in the recently used file list since it was the last file you worked on. By default, this list displays a maximum of four recently used files.

8 Choose **File**

Sen*d* To ▶
Proper*t*ies
1 C:\Student Data\Unit_01\My about OS

Note that the recently used file list in the File menu is the same as it appears in the New Document task pane.

Close the File menu — Click anywhere outside the menu.

9 In the New Document task pane, under Open a document, click **My about OS** — To open the file.

10 Close Word

The Search task panes

Explanation

By using the Search task panes, you can find files that meet specific search criteria. Office XP provides two Search task panes: Basic Search and Advanced Search. In both these task panes, you have to specify where you want to search—from your entire hard drive to just a particular folder—as well as which file type(s) you're looking for—from all Office files to program-specific files (for example, Word documents only).

Both Search task panes are shared across Word, PowerPoint, Excel, and Access. When you click the Search button on the Standard toolbar, the task pane opens to the type of search you last performed—Basic or Advanced. (The Basic Search task pane appears the very first time you click the Search button.) The task pane also retains the specified criteria from your last search—even when you switch programs. This makes it easy to perform the same kind of searches repeatedly (instead of starting from scratch every time).

Basic Search

You can use the Basic Search task pane (as shown in Exhibit 1-2) to perform keyword searches of entire files. For example, you want to find all Office files on your computer that contain a particular word. Here's how you do it:

1 Display the Basic Search task pane. To do so, click the Search button on the Standard toolbar or select Search from the task pane list. If the Advanced Search task pane appears, click Basic Search (at the bottom of the task pane).

2 Under Search, in the Search text box, enter the text you want to look for.

3 Under Other Search Options, in the Search in list, verify that My Computer is checked.

4 Under Other Search Options, in the Results should be list, verify that Office Files is checked.

5 Click Search. After a moment, the Search Results task pane will appear, displaying a list of Office files on your computer that contain the specified text. To open a file in its parent program, simply click the file name.

If you enter two or more words in the Search text box, the search utility will find files that contain any one of the specified words.

Exhibit 1-2: The Basic Search task pane

Do it!

A-4: Using the Basic Search task pane

Here's how	Here's why
1 Start Excel	
Clear **Show at startup**	At the bottom of the task pane.
2 Click 🔍	(The Search button is on the Standard toolbar.) To display the Basic Search task pane, as shown in Exhibit 1-2.
3 In the Search text box, enter **Outlander Spices**	By entering these keywords, you'll find files that contain the word "Outlander" or "Spices" (or both).

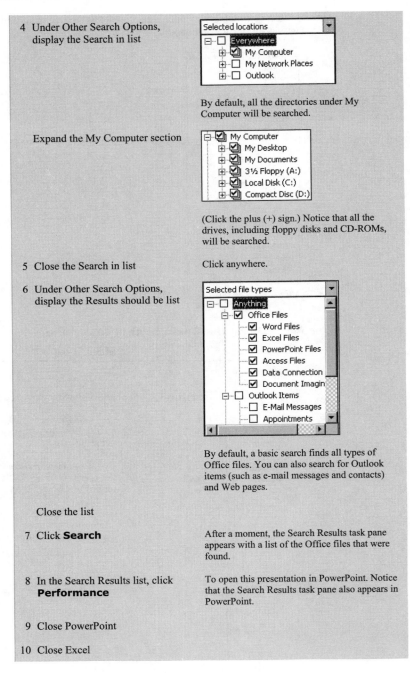

4 Under Other Search Options, display the Search in list

By default, all the directories under My Computer will be searched.

Expand the My Computer section

(Click the plus (+) sign.) Notice that all the drives, including floppy disks and CD-ROMs, will be searched.

5 Close the Search in list

Click anywhere.

6 Under Other Search Options, display the Results should be list

By default, a basic search finds all types of Office files. You can also search for Outlook items (such as e-mail messages and contacts) and Web pages.

Close the list

7 Click **Search**

After a moment, the Search Results task pane appears with a list of the Office files that were found.

8 In the Search Results list, click **Performance**

To open this presentation in PowerPoint. Notice that the Search Results task pane also appears in PowerPoint.

9 Close PowerPoint

10 Close Excel

The Advanced Search task pane

Explanation

Compared to the Basic Search task pane, you can use the Advanced Search task pane (as shown in Exhibit 1-3) to specify a wider range of search criteria. In addition to searching by keyword, you can also search by file size, file name, author, revision number, creation date, template type, and dozens of other parameters.

What's more, you can narrow or widen your search by combining parameters into complex criteria. For example, you can search for all the presentations that were modified in the last two days and whose file names contain the words "product launch." To do this kind of search, you must use the "And" option to combine parameters. You can also use the "Or" option to broaden your search. For example, you can search for all the Word documents that are at least five pages long or contain at least 1,000 words.

To display the Advanced Search task pane, click the Search button on the Standard toolbar or select Search from the task pane list. If the Basic Search task pane appears, click Advanced Search (at the bottom of the task pane).

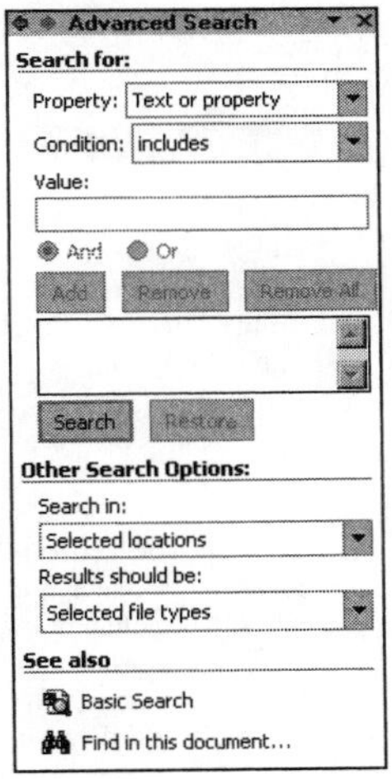

Exhibit 1-3: The Advanced Search task pane

Do it!

A-5: Using the Advanced Search task pane

Here's how	Here's why
1 Start Word	
2 Display the Basic Search task pane	Click the Search button on the Standard toolbar.
3 Under See also, click **Advanced Search**	To display the Advanced Search task pane, as shown in Exhibit 1-3.
4 Under Search for, display the Property list	

> Text or property
> Received
> Resources
> Revision
> Sent
> Size
> Start
> Status
> Subject
> Template
> Text or property

	You use this list to specify the file property or text type on which your search will be based. For example, you can search by date, revision number, file size, file name, word count, template type, and so on.
Select **File name**	You'll search for files whose names include a particular word.
5 Observe the Condition list	The default condition is "includes," which means that the search utility will look for file names that include the specified text.
6 In the Value box, enter **performance**	You'll search for Office files whose names contain the word "performance."
Click **Add**	To add the specified search criteria to the list. Advanced searches can have multiple criteria, and each one must be added to this list individually.
7 Under Other Search Options, observe the Search in and Results should be lists	Notice that they're the same as in the previous search. Namely, all directories under My Computer will be searched for all types of Office files.

8 Click **Search**	☐ My Computer (4 of 4) 🔲 Outlander performance 🔲 Performance 🔲 Sales performance 🔲 Performance
	To perform a search based on the specified criteria. After a moment, the Search Results task pane appears and displays your results.
9 Click **Modify**	To return to the Advanced Search task pane. You also know that the performance presentation you're looking for has no more than six slides. You'll add this condition to the search criteria as well.
10 From the Property list, select **Number of slides**	
From the Condition list, select **at most**	
In the Value box, enter **6**	With this combination of settings, the search utility will find presentations that have six or fewer slides.
11 Observe the indicated option	◉ And ○ Or
	By choosing And, the search utility will find files that fulfill both criteria. (If you choose Or, it will find files that fulfill either criterion.)
Add the new criteria to the list	(Click Add.) Notice that the previous search criteria remains. With this combination, the search utility will look for presentations whose file names include the word "performance" and that contain six or fewer slides.
12 Perform the search	After a moment, just one presentation, Sales performance, is found.
Open Sales performance	Notice that the presentation contains only six slides, thereby fulfilling the second search criteria.
13 Close PowerPoint	
Close the Search Results task pane	In Word.

Topic B: Using smart tags

Explanation

Office XP's *smart tags* feature provides quick and easy access to frequently used options and commands. In a way, smart tags are programmed to anticipate what you're most likely to need in certain situations. By using the smart tags, you can also perform actions that would otherwise require you to open other programs.

To work with smart tags, you use three types of buttons: Smart Tag Actions, Paste Options, and AutoCorrect Options. One of these buttons appears automatically when you perform an action that might require its use. For example, when you paste Excel data into a Word document, the Paste Options button appears automatically. You can use this button to specify exactly how you want the data to be inserted (for example, as a link).

The Smart Tag Actions button

Thanks to the smart tags feature, Office XP will recognize certain words and numbers in your documents and provide several convenient options. For example, Word will automatically highlight (with a dotted purple underline) all dates, times, addresses, place names, and recent Outlook e-mail recipients. When you point to any such underlined text, the Smart Tag Actions button will appear. You can then use this button to perform common tasks. For example, you can point to a recognized date and use the Smart Tag Actions button to open your Outlook Calendar to that date.

To change the items that an Office program will recognize with smart tags, use the AutoCorrect dialog box. Here's how:

1 Choose Tools, AutoCorrect options to open the AutoCorrect dialog box.

2 Activate the Smart Tags tab (as shown in Exhibit 1-4). Please note that the contents of this tab will vary depending on which program you're working in.

3 Under Recognizers, check those items that you want to be recognized automatically.

4 Click OK to close the dialog box.

Exhibit 1-4: The AutoCorrect dialog box in Word

Do it!

B-1: Using the Smart Tag Actions button

Here's how	Here's why
1 Open OS letter	You'll use the Smart Tag Actions button to create an Outlook contact from within this Word document.
2 Choose **Tools, AutoCorrect Options...**	To open the AutoCorrect dialog box.
3 Click the **Smart Tags** tab	Under Recognizers, notice that Word's smart tag feature is configured to recognize five types of text: dates, times, addresses, places, and recent Outlook e-mail recipients.
4 Check Label text with smart tags	(If necessary.)
5 Under Recognizers, check **Person names (English)**	With this setting, Word will also recognize names of people (first and last).
Under Recognizers, check **Telephone numbers (English)**	So that Word will also recognize phone numbers.
Click **OK**	To save the new settings and close the dialog box.

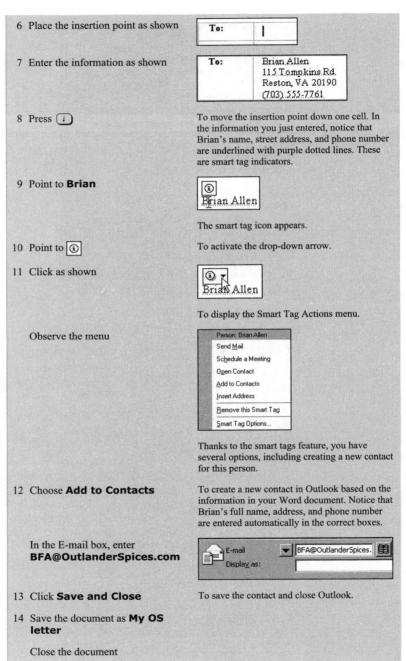

6   Place the insertion point as shown

7   Enter the information as shown

8   Press ⬇

To move the insertion point down one cell. In the information you just entered, notice that Brian's name, street address, and phone number are underlined with purple dotted lines. These are smart tag indicators.

9   Point to **Brian**

The smart tag icon appears.

10   Point to ⓘ

To activate the drop-down arrow.

11   Click as shown

To display the Smart Tag Actions menu.

Observe the menu

Thanks to the smart tags feature, you have several options, including creating a new contact for this person.

12   Choose **Add to Contacts**

To create a new contact in Outlook based on the information in your Word document. Notice that Brian's full name, address, and phone number are entered automatically in the correct boxes.

In the E-mail box, enter **BFA@OutlanderSpices.com**

13   Click **Save and Close**

To save the contact and close Outlook.

14   Save the document as **My OS letter**

Close the document

The AutoCorrect Options button

Explanation

When you point to a word that has been corrected automatically, a thin blue rectangle will appear under the first letter. Pointing to this rectangle activates the AutoCorrect Options button. To undo the automatic correction, click the button and choose the appropriate option from the shortcut menu. You can opt to undo only the current correction, or you can stop this type of correction from being made in the future. You can also use this menu to open the AutoCorrect Options dialog box.

Do it!

B-2:   Using the AutoCorrect Options button

Here's how	Here's why
1 Open OS spices	
2 Type **outlander spices**	(At the beginning of the document.) Notice that Word automatically capitalizes the letter "o." This is because it assumes that "outlander" is the first word in a sentence.
3 Point to **Outlander**	**Outlander**
	A blue rectangle appears below the first letter of the word to indicate that the word was automatically corrected.
Point to the blue rectangle	To activate the AutoCorrect Options button.
4 Click 🔻	**Outlander** spices ↶ Undo Automatic Capitalization Stop Auto-capitalizing First Letter of Sentences Control AutoCorrect Options... and being blended in small batches you can be as
	You can choose to undo only the current correction, or you can reconfigure Word to stop capitalizing the first letter of each sentence automatically.
5 Choose **Undo Automatic Capitalization**	To undo the correction in only this case. Word will continue to auto-capitalize the first word in each sentence as you type.
6 Display the AutoCorrect Options menu	Point to "outlander," point to the blue rectangle, and then click the AutoCorrect Options button.
Choose **Redo Automatic Capitalization**	Notice that the letter "O" is again capitalized.
7 Save the document as **My OS spices**	
8 Close the document	

The Paste Options button

When you copy and paste data from another page, file, or program, the Paste Options button will appear. This button provides quick and easy access to commands associated with the current paste action. For example, if you copy a bold heading and paste it into a normal paragraph, you can use the Paste Options button to specify whether the source formatting should be maintained. In this case, you can also use the Paste Options button to display the Styles and Formatting task pane.

You can also use the Paste Options button to link Excel data to a Word document. Here's how it works:

1   Open the source worksheet.

2   Copy the data that you want to appear in the destination Word document.

3   Open the destination Word document.

4   Paste the data in the desired location. The Paste Options button appears.

5   Click the Paste Options button to display the Paste Options menu.

6   Choose an appropriate option: "Keep Source Formatting and Link to Excel" or "Match Destination Table Style and Link to Excel."

Please note, however, that this linking method can be used when you're inserting only Excel data in a Word document.

Do it!

B-3:   Using the Paste Options button

Here's how	Here's why
1 Start Excel	
2 Open Sales details	In the current unit folder.
3 Copy A1:D14	You'll paste the selected cells in a Word document.
4 Create a blank Word document	
5 Choose **Edit, Paste**	The data is inserted as a table, and the Paste Options button appears near the lower-right corner of the table.
6 Point to 📋	In the document. To activate the down arrow.
Click 📋 ▾	⦿ Keep Source Formatting ○ Match Destination Table Style ○ Keep Text Only ○ Keep Source Formatting and Link to Excel ○ Match Destination Table Style and Link to Excel 🖎 Apply Style or Formatting...
	By default, Word maintains the formatting of the Excel worksheet. You can also apply Word's default table style or insert the data as raw text. In addition, you can use this menu to create a link between the source workbook and the destination document.
Choose **Keep Source Formatting and Link to Excel**	To maintain the formatting from Excel and create a link between files.
7 Save the document as **East sales details**	
8 Close Word	
Close Excel	

Topic C: Introducing the Ask a Question box

Explanation

The Help feature of Office XP, which is shared across the Office suite, contains several ways to get help. One of these ways is by using the Ask a Question box. You can directly type a question in the box and select the desired topic from the list of available help topics.

A new way to get Help

You can quickly access Help by using the Ask a Question box. This box appears in the upper-right corner of all Office program windows. To get Help:

1 Type a question (or just some key words) in the Ask a Question box.
2 Press Enter to display a list of relevant Help topics.
3 Click the appropriate topic to display it in the Help window. Form there, you can access other Help topics by using the Contents, Answer Wizard, and Index tabs.

Do it!

C-1: Using the Ask a Question box

Here's how	Here's why
1 Start PowerPoint	
Observe the Ask a Question box	Type a question for help ▼
	In the upper-right corner of the program window (on the menu bar).
2 In the Ask a Question box, type **Creating presentations**	You'll get Help on how to create presentations.
Press (↵ ENTER)	● Apply a design template ● Create a presentation using blank slides ● About creating presentations ● Create a presentation using a design template ● About design templates ▼ See more...
	To display a list of relevant Help topics.

3 Click **See more**	To display some additional topics related to creating presentations. Notice that you also have the option of searching for information on the Web.
Click **See previous**	To return to the original list.
4 Click **Create a presentation using a design template**	To display this topic in the Microsoft PowerPoint Help window.
5 Close the Microsoft PowerPoint Help window	
6 Close PowerPoint	

Unit summary: Task panes, smart tags, and the Ask a Question box

Topic A

In this unit, you learned how to use **task panes** in Office XP. You used the task panes to **create** new files and **open existing Office files**. You also learned how to **search** by using the **Basic** and **Advanced Search task panes**.

Topic B

Next, you learned about the **smart tags**. You also learned how to use the **Smart Tag Actions**, **AutoCorrect Options**, and the **Paste Options** buttons.

Topic C

Finally, you learned how to use the **Ask a Question** box to get Help in Office XP.

Independent practice activity

1 Start Word.

2 Use the Basic Search task pane to find all the workbooks on your computer that contain the word "**cinnamon**." (*Hint*: Use the Results should be list to restrict your search to Excel workbooks only.)

3 Use the Advanced Search task pane to find all the Word documents in the Student Data folder (C:\Student Data) that:

- Are at least 10 pages long, or
- Contain at most 1,000 words, or
- Have the word "outline" in their file name.

(*Hint*: Use the Search in list to restrict your search to only the Student Data folder.)

4 Close the Advanced Search task pane.

5 Open Project team from the current unit folder.

6 At the beginning of the document, type **the project team**, and then use the AutoCorrect Options button to undo the automatic capitalization of "the."

7 Use the Smart Tag Actions button to create a new contact for **Kathy Sinclair**. Enter Kathy's e-mail address as **KTS@OutlanderSpices.com**. When you're done, save and close the Contact window.

8 Use the Ask a Question box to get Help on importing files into Word. When you're done, close the Help window.

9 Save the document as **My project team**, and then close Word.

Unit 2

Other new, shared features of Office XP

Unit time: 50 minutes

Complete this unit, and you'll know how to:

A Send an e-mail message with an introduction, and send a file for review as an e-mail attachment.

B Use the Diagram and Template Galleries.

C Work with the Clips Organizer and the Insert Clip Art task pane.

D Recover non-responsive applications.

E Show toolbar buttons on one or two rows, and use the Save My Settings Wizard to store your Office configuration.

Topic A: Sending e-mail messages

Explanation

Office XP has some new and improved messaging features that are common across most of the Office applications. For example, when you send an e-mail message from an Office program other than Outlook, you can add an introduction section. Office XP also provides a new way to send an Office file to someone else for review.

The Introduction box

When you send an e-mail from Word, you can include the contents of the current document in the body of your message. When you do so, the document is converted to an HTML format. Therefore, you're not sending the Word file itself but rather an HTML version that can be viewed directly in Outlook (or any other e-mail program that can handle HTML, such as Netscape Messenger). What's new in Office XP is that an Introduction box appears in the message window wherein you can enter brief information about the included file.

Here's what you do:

1. Open the Word document, Excel worksheet, or PowerPoint slide that you want to send in the body of an e-mail message.
2. Choose File, Send To, Mail Recipient to activate the integrated e-mail components of the parent program.
3. Address the message as desired by using the To, Cc, and Subject boxes. By default, the file name is entered in the Subject box.
4. Enter the desired text in the Introduction box. This text will appear at the beginning of the message.
5. In Word, click Send a Copy. In Excel, click Send this Sheet. In PowerPoint, click Send this Slide.

When you perform the final step, the e-mail message is added to your Outbox. If Outlook is closed, then you need to start Outlook in order to transmit the message.

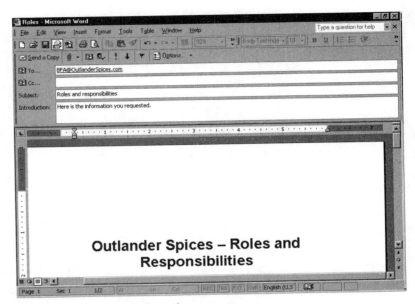

Exhibit 2-1: Word's integrated e-mail components

Do it!

A-1: Sending an e-mail with an introduction

Here's how	Here's why
1 Start Word	
2 Open Roles	(From the current unit folder.) You'll send the contents of this Word document in the body of an e-mail message. To do so, you'll use some Outlook components that have been integrated into Word.
3 Choose **File, Send To, Mail Recipient**	To activate the integrated e-mail components of Word. These appear below the Standard toolbar and above the document.
4 In the To box, enter **BFA@OutlanderSpices.com**	
5 Edit the Subject box to read **Roles and responsibilities**	Notice that the document's file name is automatically entered in the Subject box.
In the Introduction box, enter **Here is the information you requested.**	Please note that the Introduction box can accommodate much longer messages than this.

6 Click **Send a Copy**	Because Outlook is currently closed, the message is not transmitted immediately.
7 Close Word	If you're prompted to save changes, click No.
8 Start Outlook	(Maximize the window, if necessary.) Because Outlook is set to send e-mail messages later, your message is automatically moved to the Outbox folder under Messages.
9 Choose **View, Folder List**	To view the folders list.
Expand Outlook Today	If necessary.
10 In the folders list, click **Outbox**	The sent e-mail appears in the Outbox.
Open the e-mail message	The document's contents are displayed in the body of the message. Notice that the font and paragraph formatting of the original document have been maintained. The introduction text is added at the beginning of the message.
Observe the title bar	✉ Roles and responsibilities - Message (HTML) It indicates that the message is in HTML format.
11 Close the message window	
Close Outlook	

Sending documents for review

Explanation

In a work environment, you often need to send documents for review. To do this you need to set up a review cycle. A *review cycle* involves sending a document for review, reviewing a document, accepting or rejecting the suggested changes, and ending the review. Office XP provides you with the feature of sending any document for review as an attachment.

In Excel, you have the option of sharing an original document for multi-user review. To do this, choose Tools, Share Workbook. Check the option, Allow changes by more than one user at the same time. Remember to remove the share after you receive the reviewed document.

To send a document for review:

1 Open the document.

2 Choose File, Send To, Mail Recipient (for Review), to open a new message window. By default, the subject lines reads, "Please review '<file name>'." In the message body, the phrase "Please review the attached document" is automatically inserted.

3 In the To box, enter the reviewer's e-mail address.

4 Click Send.

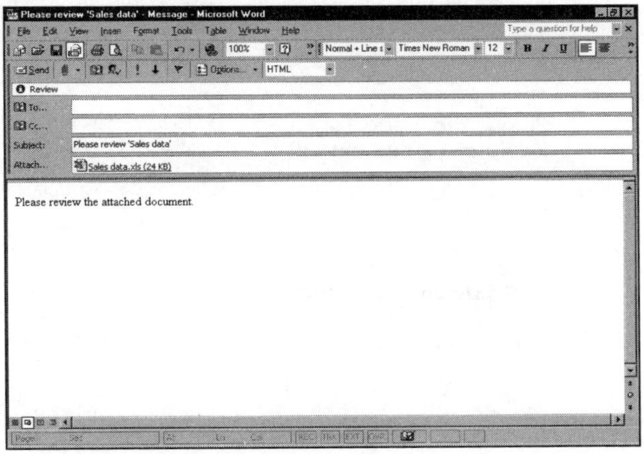

Exhibit 2-2: Sending a file for review

Do it!

A-2:   Sending an Excel worksheet for review

Here's how	Here's why
1 Start Excel	
2 Open Sales data	(From the current unit folder.) You'll send this file for review.
3 Choose **Tools, Share Workbook...**	To open the Share Workbook dialog box. By default, the Editing tab is activated.
Check **Allow changes by more than one user at the same time. This also allows workbook merging.**	This option enables multi-user review.
Click **OK**	A message box appears informing you that the file will be saved.
Click **OK**	To close the message box.
4 Observe the title bar	Microsoft Excel - Sales data [Shared] Note that the worksheet is shared for multiple use.
5 Choose **File, Send To, Mail Recipient (for Review)...**	To create a new message with the current file attached. By default, the subject line reads "Please review 'Sales data'," and "Please review the attached document" is inserted in the message body.
6 In the To box, enter **KTS@OutlanderSpices.com**	
7 Click **Send**	To send the message and close the message window.
8 Close Excel	If you're prompted to save changes, click No.

Topic B: Introducing the Diagram and Template Galleries

Explanation

Sometimes the best way to present information is in the form of a diagram. Instead of creating your diagrams from scratch, you can use one of the six templates provided by Office XP's Diagram Gallery. These templates will give you a head start in constructing organization charts and several other common diagram types, including cycle, target, radial, Venn, and pyramid. Please note that the Diagram Gallery is available only in Word, PowerPoint, and Excel. You can also create documents based on templates by using the Template Gallery.

The Diagram Gallery

To open the Diagram Gallery dialog box, choose Insert, Diagram (or click the Insert Diagram or Organization Chart button on the Drawing toolbar). This dialog box contains six icons, each of which represents a diagram type, as described in the following table.

Icon	Type	Use this type of diagram to show...
	Organization Chart	Hierarchical relationships among members of an organization.
	Cycle Diagram	Steps in a continuous process.
	Radial Diagram	Relationships of different elements of a process to a core element.
	Pyramid Diagram	Foundation-based relationships for a process.
	Venn Diagram	Areas of overlap between and among elements for a process.
	Target Diagram	Steps leading to a goal.

Do it!

B-1:   Exploring the Diagram Gallery

Here's how	Here's why
1 Start Excel	
2 Choose **View, Toolbars, Drawing**	To open the Drawing toolbar.
3 Click [icon]	(The Insert Diagram or Organization Chart button is on the Drawing toolbar.) To open the Diagram Gallery dialog box. Notice that the Organization Chart icon is selected by default and its description appears at the bottom of the dialog box.
4 Click [icon]	To read a description of the Cycle Diagram option.
5 Click the other diagram icons and read their descriptions	
6 Click **Cancel**	To close the Diagram Gallery dialog box.
7 Close Excel	

Organization charts

Explanation

You can use an *organization chart* to graphically display the hierarchical structure of an organization. You can add different levels to the chart and enhance it by highlighting the key levels.

When you insert an organization chart into your document a chart template is displayed which contains several boxes. By default, the template shows two levels of boxes. The topmost box is at level 1 and the boxes directly below it are at level 2. You can enter text into a box by selecting the box and typing the text. When you insert a diagram the Organization Chart toolbar also appears. You can use the toolbar to add additional shapes to the existing ones.

You can add different types of shapes in an organization chart, such as Coworker, Subordinate, and Assistant. The topmost shape is the Superior shape, and you can add shapes below it. A Subordinate shape is added below the currently active shape, whereas the Coworker shape is added next to the currently active shape.

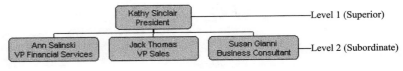

Exhibit 2-3: A sample organization chart

Do it!

B-2:   Inserting an organization chart

Here's how	Here's why
1 Start PowerPoint	
2 Choose **Format, Slide Layout...**	To display the Slide Layout task pane.
3 In the Slide Layout task pane, under Content Layouts, click as shown	
	To apply a blank layout to the current slide.
Close the Slide Layout task pane	
4 Open the Diagram Gallery dialog box	(Click Insert Diagram or Organization Chart on the Drawing toolbar.) Notice that the Organization Chart icon is selected by default.
5 Click **OK**	Notice that a blank organization chart with four shapes is inserted in the slide and the Organization Chart toolbar appears.
6 Click the top shape	
	To activate the insertion point. You'll enter some text here.
Type **Kathy Sinclair**	This is the name of the project leader.
Press (← ENTER)	
7 Type **President**	This is the project leader's title.
Deselect the box	Notice that this shape automatically increases in size to accommodate the text.

8 Enter text in the remaining shapes,
   as shown in Exhibit 2-3

   Deselect the organization chart

9 Select the indicated shape

10 Display the Insert Shape menu   On the Organization Chart toolbar.

   Choose **Subordinate**

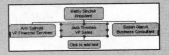

To create a subordinate under Jack Thomas. A
box appears at level 3 in the chart.

11 Select the new shape

12 From the Insert Shape menu,   To insert another shape at the same level. Both
   choose **Coworker**   of these shapes represent subordinates of Jack
                                        Thomas.

   In the two new shapes, enter the
   indicated text

13 Save the presentation as **My**   In the current unit folder.
   organization chart

   Close PowerPoint

Pyramid diagrams

Explanation

You use the pyramid diagram to show relationships that are foundation-based. For example, you can use this type of diagram to show the flow of information in an organization, as shown in Exhibit 2-4.

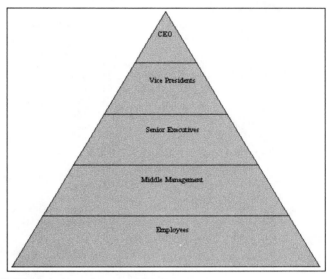

Exhibit 2-4: A sample pyramid diagram

Do it!

B-3: Inserting a pyramid diagram

Here's how	Here's why
1 Start Word	
2 Open Team summary	(From the current unit folder.) You'll create a pyramid diagram for Outlander Spices in this Word document.
Place the insertion point as shown	**Susan Gianni, Business Consultant** Susan will analyze our business proce: I You'll have to scroll to the end of the document.
3 Insert a blank pyramid diagram	(Open the Diagram Gallery dialog box, select the Pyramid Diagram icon, and click OK.) Notice that the blank pyramid diagram has three levels to start with. Also, the Diagram toolbar appears.

4 Click as shown

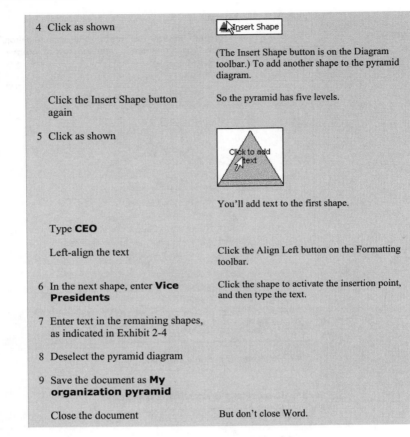

(The Insert Shape button is on the Diagram toolbar.) To add another shape to the pyramid diagram.

Click the Insert Shape button again

So the pyramid has five levels.

5 Click as shown

You'll add text to the first shape.

Type **CEO**

Left-align the text

Click the Align Left button on the Formatting toolbar.

6 In the next shape, enter **Vice Presidents**

Click the shape to activate the insertion point, and then type the text.

7 Enter text in the remaining shapes, as indicated in Exhibit 2-4

8 Deselect the pyramid diagram

9 Save the document as **My organization pyramid**

Close the document

But don't close Word.

The Template Gallery

Explanation

Office XP provides a host of new templates across all the Office applications. The Template Gallery is a collection of the latest templates categorized and available on the Web. You can preview or download a particular template from the Web and create new documents, spreadsheets, and presentations based on it. Microsoft keeps updating its database of available templates on the Web site http://www.microsoft.com/TemplateGallery.

To create a new Office file by using the Template Gallery:

1 Open the New task pane in any application.

2 Under New from template, click Templates on Microsoft.com. The first time you do this, Internet Explorer opens to Microsoft's Office Update Worldwide Web page, where you specify the region of the world in which you work. After you do so, the Template Gallery page is displayed.

3 Using the category links, navigate to the desired template. (You can also search by keyword.) To preview a template, use the Go to Preview link.

4 Click the Edit button to create a new file based on the selected template.

Do it!

B-4: Working with the Template Gallery

Here's how	Here's why
1 Display the New Document task pane	Choose File, New.
2 Under New from template, click **Templates on Microsoft.com**	To start Internet Explorer and go directly to Microsoft's Template Gallery page, an online collection of Office templates of all types.
3 Click **Marketing**	To display the sub-categories of Marketing templates.
4 Click **Presentations**	To display the presentation templates.
5 Click **Selling a product or service**	To display a page containing an outline for the selected PowerPoint template. Notice that the preview doesn't show you the template's layout or graphic content.
Click **Accept**	(Scroll down to the bottom of the page.) The detailed information on the selected template appears.
6 Click **Edit in Microsoft PowerPoint**	The Microsoft Office Template Gallery progress bar appears indicating the percentage of the template being downloaded. A new presentation is created in PowerPoint, based on the new template.
7 Close PowerPoint	
Close the browser window	

Topic C: **Working with clip art**

Explanation

A way to add visual appeal to your Office files is to insert clip art. The term clip art refers to pre-designed pictures and other graphics that can be inserted into Office files to give them more visual impact. The Microsoft Clip Gallery contains hundreds of clip art organized into categories, such as Business, Communications, Food & Dining, and Nature, to name just a few. You can use clip art in presentations, workbooks, e-mail messages, and Word documents.

Organizing clips

The first time you insert a clip art object, you will be prompted to activate the Microsoft Clip Organizer. The Clip Organizer automatically catalogs and indexes all of your picture, sound, and motion clips. This tool makes it easier to find the clip you're looking for, either by browsing or through a keyword search. When all the clips are organized, the Microsoft Clip Organizer window opens with a browser-like interface. You can click and preview the thumbnails of clips found in the respective folders.

The next time you want to add clips, you can use the Clip Organizer as follows:

1 In the Insert Clip Art task pane, click Clip Organizer, to open the Microsoft Clip Organizer window.

2 Choose File, Add Clips to Organizer, Automatically.

3 Click OK.

Do it!

C-1: **Using the Microsoft Clip Organizer**

Here's how	Here's why
1 Start PowerPoint	
2 Click 🖻	(The Insert Clip Art button is on the Drawing toolbar.) Because this is the first time you're inserting a clip art object, the Add Clips to Organizer message box appears prompting you to activate the Microsoft Clip Organizer. The Clip Organizer automatically catalogs all picture, sound, and motion clips on your computer, making it easier to find the clip you're looking for.
3 Click **Now**	To catalog all of the clip art files stored on your hard disk. The progress bar appears, indicating that the clips are being organized. When this process is completed, the progress bar disappears.
Under See also, click **Clip Organizer**	To open the Favorites - Microsoft Clip Organizer window.
4 Under My Collections, double-click **Student Data**	To display this folder's subfolders.

5 Under Student Data, click the current unit folder	To display the clips stored in this folder in the right pane.
6 Close the Microsoft Clip Organizer window	
7 Close the presentation	But don't close PowerPoint.

Inserting clip art

Explanation

The procedure for inserting clip art is the same across all Office programs. No matter which program you use, the same collection of clip art is available to you via the Clip Organizer, which contains dozens of pictures, sounds, and motion clips. You can index the clips stored on your machine and search for specific clips based on a keyword, file format, file name, or clip collection. A *clip collection* is a set of media clips organized in a hierarchical structure.

To insert a clip art in a presentation or Word document:

1 Choose Insert, Picture, Clip Art to open the Insert Clip Art task pane.

2 In the Search text box, enter a keyword.

3 Click Search.

4 From the Results box, select the clip you want to insert.

Please note that you can insert clip art in an e-mail message only if you use Word as your e-mail editor.

Do it!

C-2: Using the Insert Clip Art task pane

Here's how	Here's why
1 Open Vision	(From the current unit folder.) You'll insert a clip in this presentation.
2 Move to the third slide	(On the Outline tab, click Our Vision.) You'll insert a clip into this slide.
3 Under Search for, in the Search text box, enter **telescope**	
4 Click **Search**	The thumbnails of clips related to the keyword, Future appears in the Insert Clip Art task pane.
5 Click as shown	To insert the clip in the slide.
6 Save the presentation as **My vision**	

Topic D: Application recovery

Explanation

Office XP's Application Recovery tool reduces the risk that you'll lose data when an Office program stops responding.

Recovering data from non-responsive applications

Sometimes an Office application will stop responding ("freeze" or "hang") for no apparent reason. With previous versions of Office, you had no choice but to end the task (for example, by pressing Ctrl+Alt+Delete), which would most likely result in the loss of your most recent changes. With Office XP's new Microsoft Office Application Recovery tool, you can attempt to restart the non-responsive application, thereby reducing the risk of lost data (and wasted time).

The Application Recovery tool doesn't necessarily work every time you use it. Its effectiveness depends on the source and extent of the problem that caused your application(s) to stop responding. Also, the Application Recovery tool will only work with Office programs.

To use this tool, choose Start, Programs, Microsoft Office Tools, Microsoft Office Application Recovery. In the Microsoft Office Application Recovery window, you can click End Application to close a non-responsive application or click Recover Application to restart the application and recover data. The Restart Application button might appear instead of the Recover Application button, depending on the application that's selected. But, both the buttons do the exact same thing. After you recover a non-responding application, you should save your data immediately, close the application(s) properly, and restart your computer.

AutoRecover

You can also use the AutoRecover feature to prevent data loss when an application stops responding. This feature is activated by default, and you can increase or decrease the frequency with which each Office program automatically stores your most recent changes. To do so:

1   Start any Office program.

2   Open the Options dialog box.

3   Verify that Save AutoRecover information is checked.

4   Set the time duration after which it should take place.

When you recover a document, the AutoRecover information that was stored last is recovered. So, it's advisable to increase the frequency of saving the AutoRecover information. By using the AutoRecover option, you have the choice to discard the recovered file, save it and replace the original, or save it as a separate file. Note that storing the AutoRecover information is not the same as saving a file. AutoRecover stores your changes only temporarily, so they will be lost if you close the file without saving it. (Save the file by clicking the Save button, pressing Ctrl+S, or choosing File, Save).

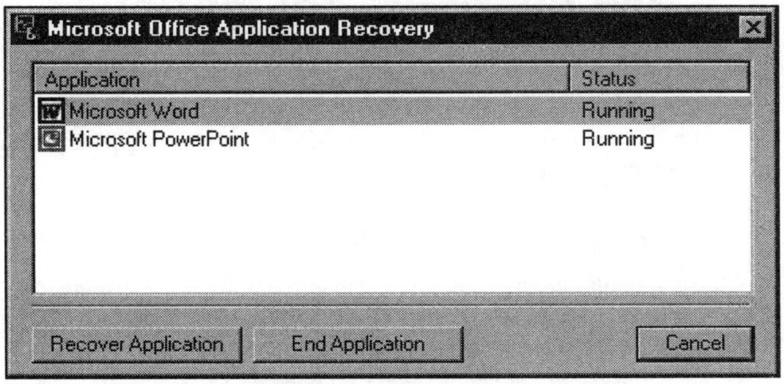

Exhibit 2-5: The Microsoft Office Application Recovery window

Do it!

D-1: Recovering data from non-responsive applications

Here's how	Here's why
1 Verify that Word and PowerPoint are running	
2 Choose **Start, Programs, Microsoft Office Tools, Microsoft Office Application Recovery**	To open the Microsoft Office Application Recovery window. Notice that both the active Office applications, Word and PowerPoint, appear in the Application list, as shown in Exhibit 2-5. This window shows the status of all the applications is Running. If an application stops responding, the entry in the Status column would change to Not Responding.
Observe the indicated buttons	
	You can use the Recover Application button to restart the non-responsive application and recover data from it. You use the End Application button to close the non-responsive applications without trying to save your most recent changes.
3 Click **Cancel**	To close the Microsoft Office Application Recovery window.
4 Close PowerPoint	
Close Word	

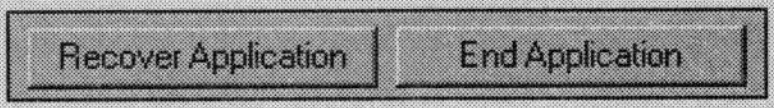

Topic E: New configuration options

Explanation

Office XP introduces several new configuration options, two of which you'll learn about in this topic. First, you'll learn a quick and easy way to show toolbar buttons on one or two rows. You'll also learn how to store your Office settings for transfer to another computer.

The Toolbar Options button

By default, the Standard and Formatting toolbars are displayed as a single row of buttons in Excel, Word, and PowerPoint. This is to conserve screen space so you have more room to work. However, some toolbar buttons are hidden in this configuration, so you might want to display these toolbars on two rows. To do so, click the Toolbar Options button (at the end of either toolbar) to display the shortcut menu, and then choose Show Buttons on Two Rows. To go back to a one-row configuration, clicking the Toolbar Options button again and choose Show Buttons on One Row.

The Customize dialog box

Another way to change the configuration of these toolbars is by using the Customize dialog box. Here's how it works:

1   Right-click either toolbar to display the shortcut menu.

2   Choose Customize to open the Customize dialog box. By default, the Options tab is activated.

3   Under Personalized Menus and Toolbars, check or clear Show Standard and Formatting toolbars on two rows.

4   Click Close.

Do it!

E-1: Showing toolbar buttons on one or two rows

Here's how	Here's why
1 Start Word	By default, the Standard and Formatting toolbars are displayed as a single row of buttons. However, due to limited space on the row, several buttons are hidden from view.
2 Click ⯮	(The Toolbar Options button is at end of the Formatting toolbar.) To display the shortcut menu.
Choose **Show Buttons on Two Rows**	To separate the Standard and Formatting toolbar in two rows. Note that the Formatting toolbar appears below the Standard toolbar.
3 Right-click any toolbar	(Anywhere will do.) To display the shortcut menu.
4 Choose **Customize...**	To open the Customize dialog box. By default, the Options tab is activated.
5 Under Personalized Menus and Toolbars, clear **Show Standard and Formatting toolbars on two rows**	
Click **Close**	The toolbars appear as before.
6 Close Word	

The Save My Settings Wizard

Explanation

You can use the Save My Settings Wizard to save your current Office configuration to a single file, which you can then use to quickly configure Office on another computer. This wizard also makes it possible for multiple users to alternate using the same computer with different Office configurations.

To store your Office configuration to a file:

1 Choose Start, Programs, Microsoft Office Tools, Save My Settings Wizard to display the first step of the wizard. To proceed, click Next.

2 Verify that Save the settings from this Machine is selected. To proceed, click Next.

3 Select Save the settings to a File. In the text box, a default file path is automatically entered. To specify a different path, you can type it or use the Browse button.

4 Click Finish to save your settings to the specified file.

To restore your settings from a file, you use basically the same procedure, except you select Restore previously saved settings to this machine in step 2.

Do it!

E-2:   Saving your Office configuration to a file

Here's how	Here's why
1 Choose **Start, Programs, Microsoft Office Tools, Save My Settings Wizard**	To start the wizard.
Click **Next**	To move to the next step in the Wizard.
2 Verify that Save the settings from this machine is selected	By selecting this option, your Office configuration will be saved to a single file.
Click **Next**	
3 Select **Save the settings to a File**	You'll save your configuration to a folder on your hard drive. In the text box, notice that the wizard automatically inserts a suggested file path.
Click **Browse**	To open the Save As dialog box.
4 Navigate to the current unit folder	You'll store your settings file in this folder.
Edit the File name box to read **My settings**	
Observe the Save as type box	All Office settings files are saved with the .ops extension.
Click **Save**	To return to the wizard. Notice that the specified path is inserted in the text box.
5 Click **Finish**	To save the settings file.
6 Click **Exit**	To close the wizard.

Unit summary: Other new, shared features of Office XP

Topic A   In this unit, you learned how to send an Office file to an e-mail recipient along with an **introduction**. You also learned how to send Office **files for review**.

Topic B   Next, you examined the Diagram Gallery. You learned how to create **organization charts** and **pyramid diagrams**. You also learned how to download the latest templates from **Microsoft's Template Gallery Web page**.

Topic C   Next, you learned how to **organize** clips and media files by using the **Microsoft Clip Organizer**. Then, you learned how to insert clips by using the **Insert Clip Art task pane**.

Topic D   Then, you learned how to **recover non-responsive applications** by using the **Microsoft Office Application Recovery** tool.

Topic E   Finally, you learned how use the **Toolbar Options button** to configure the Standard and Formatting toolbars. You also saved your Office settings to a file by using the Save My Settings Wizard.

Independent practice activity

1 Start PowerPoint and open First presentation.

2 Move to the Payment slide (#3) and insert a Venn diagram.

3 Add a fourth circle to the Venn diagram.

4 Move to the Delivery slide (#4) and insert a clip art image of a race car. (*Hint*: In the Insert Clip Art task pane, enter the search term "race car.")

5 Close the Insert Clip Art task pane and save the presentation as **My presentation**.

6 Send the presentation for review to **JPM@OutlanderSpices.com**.

7 Close the presentation and close PowerPoint.

8 Start Word and display the Standard and Formatting toolbars on two rows. When you're done, close Word.

9 Use the Save My Settings Wizard to restore your Office configuration from the **My settings** file (in the current unit folder).

Unit 3

What's new in Word 2002

Unit time: 90 minutes

Complete this unit, and you'll know how to:

A Work with the formatting task panes, and use new methods to format multiple selections, bullets, and tables.

B Use the Word Count toolbar and apply watermarks to your documents.

Topic A: **Working with formatting features**

Explanation

When it comes to document formatting, Word 2002 offers several new features and options. First, there are two task panes found exclusively in Word: Styles and Formatting and Reveal Formatting. Word also provides you with new ways to format multiple selections, bullets, and tables.

The Styles and Formatting task pane

You can use the Styles and Formatting task pane to view, create, and reapply styles in your documents. To display this task pane, choose Format, Styles and Formatting.

The task pane provides you with the following options:

- View the style applied to the selected text.
- Apply different styles by using the Pick formatting to apply list.
- Create new styles by clicking the New Style button.
- Simultaneously select multiple text passages with matching formatting by clicking the Select All button.

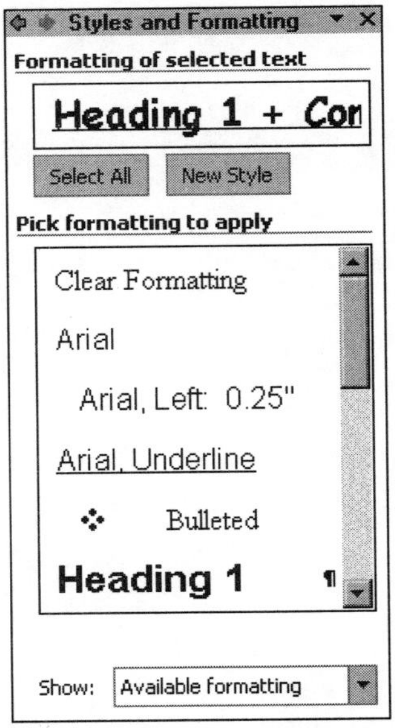

Exhibit 3-1: The Styles and Formatting task pane

Do it!

A-1:   Using the Styles and Formatting task pane

Here's how	Here's why
1 Start Word	
2 Open Products	From the current unit folder.
3 Select **Hot Sauces**	You'll view and change the formatting of this heading by using the Styles and Formatting task pane.
4 Click	

(The Styles and Formatting button is on the Formatting toolbar.) To display the Styles and Formatting task pane. The formatting styles of the selected text appear in the Formatting of selected text box.

5 From the Pick formatting to apply list, select the indicated style	

To apply a slightly different style to the selected text. Notice that the line spacing changes.

| Deselect the text | Click anywhere. |
| 6 Select the indicated bullet item | |

You'll use the Select All button to select all of the text in this document that has the same formatting as the selected words.

7 In the Styles and Formatting task pane, click **Select All**	To select the matching text.
From the Font Size list, select **14**	Note that the formatting is applied to the selected text simultaneously. You can also apply similar formatting by using the Format Painter button. But using the task pane can save you time and effort.
Deselect the text	
8 Click [🅰]	To close the Styles and Formatting task pane.
9 Save the document as **My products**	In the current unit folder.

The Reveal Formatting task pane

Explanation

The Reveal Formatting task pane shows the formatting information of the text in your document. It displays the current font and paragraph formatting of the selected text. You can easily update these properties from the task pane itself.

To open the Reveal Formatting task pane (as shown in Exhibit 3-2) choose Format, Reveal Formatting. When you select text in your document, its formatting information is displayed in the task pane. To modify the formatting of the selected text, click the appropriate property link (in blue) to open the associated dialog box. For example, if you click Font, the Font dialog box opens so you can change the font of the selected text.

You can also format a text selection as its surrounding text. To do this you need to click the arrow in the Selected text box and select Apply Formatting of Surrounding text. To remove formatting from the selected text, check Clear Formatting.

You can also compare the formatting of two text selections. To do so, select the text, check the Compare to another selection box, and then select the text to be compared. The result of the comparison appears in the Formatting differences box.

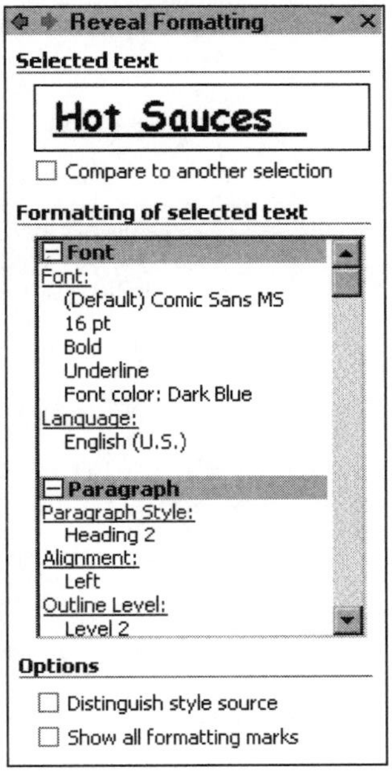

Exhibit 3-2: The Reveal Formatting task pane

Do it!

A-2: Using the Reveal Formatting task pane

Here's how	Here's why
1 Choose **Format**, **Reveal Formatting...**	To open the Reveal Formatting task pane. It contains the font, paragraph, and section information about the selected text.
2 Select **Hot Sauces**	The formatting of the selected text is revealed in the Reveal Formatting task pane, as shown in Exhibit 3-2.
3 Click as shown	 To open the Font dialog box.
4 From the Font list, select **Arial Black**	
Click **OK**	To change the font.

5 In the Reveal Formatting task pane, check **Compare to another selection**	You'll compare the formatting of two different selections. Under Selected text, a second box appears.
6 Select **Rubs and Marinades**	In the document window.
Observe the task pane	Under Formatting differences, a comparison of the two selections is displayed. In each set of properties, the first item refers to the top selection, and the second item refers to the bottom selection.
7 Open the Font dialog box	Click the Font link in the task pane.
Change the font size to 16	(From the Size list, select 16 and click OK.) In the task pane, notice that one of the formatting differences disappears. This is because both selections are now the same size.
Deselect the text	
8 Close the Reveal Formatting task pane	
9 Update the document	

Formatting multiple selections

Explanation

In previous versions of Word, you were limited to selecting only one text item at a time. With Word 2002, you can select multiple text items by holding the Ctrl key and using your mouse (the same way you select multiple files in Windows Explorer). After doing so, you can format all of the selected items simultaneously.

Do it!

A-3: Formatting multiple selections

Here's how	Here's why
1 Select **Flavorings - Oils**	You'll select and format multiple text items.
2 While holding (CTRL) , select **Hot Sauces** and **Rubs and Marinades**	When you're done, notice that all three items remain selected.
3 From the Font list, select **Comic Sans MS**	To apply the same font to all three headings.
4 Click *I*	(The Italics button is on the Formatting toolbar.) To italicize the selected text.

5 Display the Line Spacing list

On the Formatting toolbar, click the down arrow next to the Line Spacing button.

Select **1.5**

To apply the same line spacing to all three headings.

Deselect the text

6 Update the document

Formatting bullets

Explanation

When working with a bulleted list in previous versions of Word, you could not select the bullets separately from the text in the list. Now, in Word 2002, you can select all of the bullets (without the text) by simply clicking any bullet. This makes it easy to reformat your bullets without affecting the text.

Do it!

A-4: Formatting bullets in a list

Here's how	Here's why
1 Under Flavorings – Oils, click any bullet	*Flavorings - Oils* Almond Flavoring Oil Amaretto Flavoring Oil Anise Flavoring Oil Blackberry Flavor Oil Blueberry Flavoring Oil Hot Sauce Harry's Wic Pepper Ranch Hot Wir Wing-Time, BBQ Flavo Wing-Time, Garlic Flav To select all of the bullets without selecting any text. Next, you'll reformat the bullets.
2 From the Font color list, select the indicated color	Rose More Colors... To apply a new color to the bullets.

3 From the Font list, select **Marlett**	To change the shape of the bullets.
Deselect the bullets	
4 Apply the same formatting to the remaining bullets in the document	
5 Update and close the document	

Formatting tables

Explanation

You can now create tables with consistent formatting in Word by saving a set of table formatting options as a single style. Once saved, you can apply the style to any table quickly and easily by using the Table AutoFormat dialog box.

To create a new table style:

1 Choose Table, Table AutoFormat to open the Table AutoFormat dialog box.
2 Click New to open the New Style dialog box.
3 In the Name box, enter a name for the new style.
4 Set the formatting options for the new style. As you work, the dialog box displays a preview of the style.
5 Click OK to close the New Style dialog box. In the Table AutoFormat dialog box, the new style is added to the Table styles list.
6 Close the Table AutoFormat dialog box.

To apply your new style to a table:

1 Place the insertion pointer anywhere in the table.
2 Open the Table AutoFormat dialog box.
3 From the Table styles list, select your new style.
4 Click Apply.

You can also apply your custom table style by using the Styles and Formatting task pane.

Do it!

A-5: Formatting tables by using customized table styles

Here's how	Here's why
1 Open Formatting tables	You'll create a new custom style and apply it to the tables in the document.
2 Place the insertion point anywhere in the table	
3 Choose **Table, Table AutoFormat...**	To open the Table AutoFormat dialog box.
4 Click **New**	To open the New Style dialog box.

5   Edit the Name box to read **My style**

This will be the name of your custom table style.

6   Set the formatting options as indicated

Apply formatting to:	Whole table	▼
Arial	▼	11 ▼	**B** *I* U A ▼

You'll need to set the font, font size, line style, and line thickness. The indicated line style is at the very bottom of the Line Style list, so you'll have to scroll down to select it.

7   Click ⊞

(The All Borders button is under the Formatting options.) To display lines between rows and columns, as shown in the preview area.

8   Click **OK**

To close the New Style dialog box. In the Table AutoFormat dialog box, notice that "My style" is now in the Table styles list and is automatically selected.

Click **Apply**

To apply the new style to the table in which you placed the insertion point.

9   Scroll down to page 2

10   Place the insertion point in the table

(Anywhere will do.) You'll apply your new style to this table.

11   Open the Table AutoFormat dialog box

Choose Table, Table AutoFormat.

From the Table styles list, select **My style**

You might need to scroll up in the list to locate My style.

Click **Apply**

To close the dialog box and apply the style.

12   Save the document as **My formatting tables**

Close the document

Topic B: Other new features

Explanation

Word 2002 introduces the Word Count toolbar, which you can use to automatically count the number of words, characters, lines, pages, and paragraphs in your document. The new version of Word also makes it easier to apply a watermark to a document.

The Word Count toolbar

Let's say you're working on a report, and your supervisor says that it can be no longer than 1000 words. How do you keep track of exactly how much text you've written? In Word 2002, you can use new Word Count toolbar. Here's how it works:

1 Choose View, Toolbars, Word Count to display the Word Count toolbar.

2 Click Recount to count the words in the document. The total is displayed on the toolbar.

3 On the toolbar, display the Word Count Statistics list to view other information, including the total number of characters (with and without spaces), lines, pages, and paragraphs in your document.

You can also generate counts for just a portion of your document by selecting the desired section and clicking the Recount button.

Do it!

B-1: Using the Word Count toolbar

Here's how	Here's why
1 Open My products	You'll generate the word count statistics for this document.
2 Choose **View**, **Toolbars**, **Word Count**	To display the Word Count toolbar.
Click **Recount**	(On the Word Count toolbar.) To count all of the words in the entire document.
Observe the Word Count Toolbar	It indicates that the document contains 143 words.
3 Under Flavorings – Oils, select all of the bullet items	You can also count the words in just a portion of your document. To do so, select the desired section before clicking Recount.
4 Click **Recount**	The selection contains 45 words, as indicated on the toolbar.

5 Click as shown

> Word Count
> 45 Words   Recount
> Word Count Statistics

To display the Word Count Statistics list.

Observe the list

> 45 Words
> 219 Characters (no spaces)
> 268 Characters (with spaces)
> 9 Lines
> 1 Page
> 9 Paragraphs

It provides other counts for the selection, including the total number of characters, lines, pages, and paragraphs.

6 Deselect the text

Close the Word Count toolbar

7 Update the document

Working with watermarks

Explanation

A *watermark* is a picture or text that appears in the background of a document. Many companies add their logo as a watermark on their letterhead stationery. To facilitate the process of creating a watermark, Word 2002 introduces the Printed Watermark dialog box.

To create a picture-based watermark:

1 Choose Format, Background, Printed Watermark to open the Printed Watermark dialog box.

2 Select Picture watermark.

3 Click Select Picture to open the Insert Picture dialog box.

4 Navigate to the folder that contains the picture you want to insert as a watermark.

5 Select the desired picture, and then click Insert to return to the Printed Watermark dialog box.

6 Click OK to close the dialog box and apply the watermark.

You can use a similar procedure to create a text-based watermark.

Do it!

B-2:   Creating a watermark

Here's how	Here's why
1 Choose **Format, Background, Printed Watermark...**	To open the Printed Watermark dialog box.
2 Select **Picture watermark**	You'll create a watermark by inserting a picture in the background. Notice, however, that you can also use this dialog box to create a text-based watermark.
3 Click **Select Picture**	To open the Insert Picture dialog box.
4 Navigate to the current unit folder	
Select the **Spices** image	If necessary.
Click **Insert**	To return to the Printed Watermark dialog box. Notice that the path of the selected picture appears next to the Select Picture button.
5 Clear **Washout**	To prevent the picture from being faded automatically upon insertion. If the picture is too bold, you can reinsert it with this option checked.
Click **OK**	To close the dialog box and apply the watermark, which appears in the background of the document.
6 Update and close the document	

Unit summary: What's new in Word 2002

Topic A   In this unit, you learned how to use the **Styles and Formatting** and **Reveal Formatting** task panes. Then, you learned how to **format only the bullets** in a bulleted list. You also created and applied a **custom table style**. Next, you learned how to select and **format multiple text items simultaneously**.

Topic B   Finally, you used the **Word Count toolbar** to calculate text statistics for a document. You also used the **Printed Watermark** dialog box to create a picture-based **watermark** in the background of a document.

Independent practice activity

1 Open Word practice.

2 Open the Styles and Formatting task pane.

3 Use the task pane to select all of the text that has the same formatting as the heading **About us**.

4 Make the selected text bold and underlined.

5 Close the Styles and Formatting task pane.

6 Open the Reveal Formatting task pane.

7 Compare the formatting of the first and second paragraphs under the heading **About us**. Then, use the Formatting differences list to make the second paragraph match the first paragraph.

8 Make the formatting of both the paragraphs similar. (*Hint*: Under Formatting differences, click Font and change the font size of the selected text to 14.)

9 Close the Reveal Formatting task pane.

10 Use the Word Count toolbar to calculate the total number of words in the entire document (your result should be 593). When you're done, close the toolbar.

11 Create a text watermark that reads **CONFIDENTIAL**. Set this word's font formatting as Arial, 36 point, red.

12 Save the document as **My word practice**, and then close it.

13 Close Word.

Unit 4

What's new in Excel 2002

Unit time: 60 minutes

Complete this unit, and you'll know how to:

A Add colors to worksheet tabs, use the border drawing tool and AutoSum list, insert pictures in headers, e-mail a range of cells, and prevent single-column sorting.

B Use the Error Checking and Stock Quote smart tags.

C Use the Watch Window and the Evaluate Formula dialog box.

Topic A: Working with basic features

Explanation

Unlike previous versions of the program, you can do the following tasks with Excel 2002:

- Apply colors to worksheet tabs
- Draw borders around cells by dragging the mouse
- Use the AutoSum feature to apply functions other than Sum, including Average, Max, Min, and Count
- Insert a picture in a header or footer
- Prevent single-column sorting

Worksheet tab colors

You can make your workbook attractive and differentiate between worksheets by adding colors to the worksheet tabs. To do so:

1 Right-click the desired sheet tab to display the shortcut menu.
2 Choose Tab Color to open the Format Tab Color dialog box.
3 Select an appropriate color.
4 Click OK.

Do it!

A-1: Adding color to worksheet tabs

Here's how	Here's why
1 Start Excel	
2 Open Yearly sales	(From the current unit folder.) You'll add colors to the worksheet tabs.
3 Right-click the **North** worksheet tab	
	To display the shortcut menu.
Choose **Tab Color...**	To open the Format Tab Color dialog box.
4 Select a red color	Any shade will do.
Click **OK**	To apply the selected color to the active worksheet tab. Notice that a red line appears along the bottom of the tab.
5 Click the **South** worksheet tab	To activate the next worksheet. Notice that the North tab is now completely red with white lettering.

6 Apply a yellow color to the South worksheet tab	Right-click the South tab, choose Tab Color to open the Format Tab Color dialog box, select a yellow color (any shade will do), and click OK.
7 Apply three other colors to the East, West, and Report tabs	Any colors will do, but make sure that they're different from each other.
8 Save the workbook as **My yearly sales**	In the current unit folder.

The border drawing tool

Explanation

Thanks to Excel's new border drawing tool, you can apply borders to cells by dragging your mouse. Here's how it works:

To use the border drawing pencil:

1 Choose View, Toolbars, Borders to display the Borders toolbar.
2 From the Line Style list, select the desired style. The pointer changes to a pencil, indicating that the border drawing tool is activated.
3 If necessary, click the Line Color button to display the color palette, and then select the desired color.
4 Drag your mouse to draw the desired borders in your worksheet. To draw a border around a range of cells, drag the mouse as if you were selecting the range.
5 Close the Borders toolbar to deactivate the border drawing tool.

Do it!

A-2:   Working with the border drawing tool

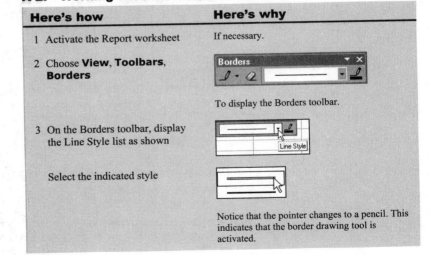

Here's how	Here's why
1 Activate the Report worksheet	If necessary.
2 Choose **View, Toolbars, Borders**	To display the Borders toolbar.
3 On the Borders toolbar, display the Line Style list as shown	
Select the indicated style	Notice that the pointer changes to a pencil. This indicates that the border drawing tool is activated.

4 Point as shown

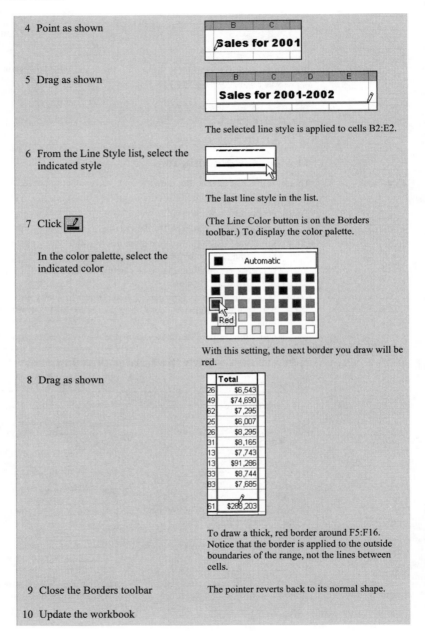

5 Drag as shown

The selected line style is applied to cells B2:E2.

6 From the Line Style list, select the indicated style

The last line style in the list.

7 Click 🖉

(The Line Color button is on the Borders toolbar.) To display the color palette.

In the color palette, select the indicated color

With this setting, the next border you draw will be red.

8 Drag as shown

To draw a thick, red border around F5:F16. Notice that the border is applied to the outside boundaries of the range, not the lines between cells.

9 Close the Borders toolbar

The pointer reverts back to its normal shape.

10 Update the workbook

The AutoSum list

Explanation

In the previous version of Excel, you could use the AutoSum button to enter the Sum function with a single click. In Excel 2002, this button has been expanded to a list that includes the Average, Count, Max, and Min functions. Here's how you use it:

1   Select the cell in which you want to enter a function.
2   Click the down arrow next to the AutoSum button to display the list.
3   Select the desired function to insert its syntax in the selected cell.
4   Use your mouse to select the desired range and insert it in the function.
5   Press Enter.

You can also select the desired range before selecting a function from the AutoSum list. When you do so, the completed function is entered in the next empty cell below or to the right of the range.

Do it!

A-3:   Working with the expanded AutoSum feature

Here's how	Here's why
1 In D17, enter **Average quarterly sales**	You'll calculate and display average sales for four quarters.
2 In D18, enter **Highest quarterly sales**	You'll identify and display the highest sales value for the four quarters.
3 Select F17	
Click as shown	
	(The AutoSum button is on the Standard toolbar.) To display the AutoSum list, which includes the Sum, Average, Count, Max, and Min functions.
Select **Average**	To insert the syntax for the Average function in cell F17. Notice that the default cell range is selected.
4 Select B16:E16	(Use your mouse.) To insert this range in the function.
Press (↵ ENTER)	To complete the formula and calculate the average value ($72,051).
5 Verify that F18 is selected	

6 From the AutoSum list, select **Max**	To insert the Max function syntax in the selected cell.
Select B16:E16	To complete the formula, which identifies and displays the highest quarterly sales figure ($76,792).
Press (↵ ENTER)	The highest sales value for the four quarters appears in F18.
7 Update the workbook	

Pictures in headers and footers

Explanation

With Excel 2002, you can insert pictures in headers and footers. For example, you can insert pictures such as company logos in the header of a worksheet. To insert a picture in the header of a worksheet:

1 Choose View, Header and Footer to open the Page Setup dialog box. By default, the Header/Footer tab is activated.

2 Click Custom Header to open the Header dialog box.

3 Place the insertion point in the section where you want the picture to appear (Left, Center, or Right).

4 Click the Insert Picture button to open the Insert Picture dialog box.

5 Navigate to and select the desired picture, and then click Insert to return to the Header dialog box.

6 Click OK to return to the Page Setup dialog box.

7 Click OK to close the dialog box.

Do it!

A-4:   Inserting a picture in a header

Here's how	Here's why
1 Choose **View**, **Header and Footer...**	To open the Page Setup dialog box. By default, the Header/Footer tab is activated.
2 Click **Custom Header**	To open the Header dialog box. By using this dialog box, you can insert page numbers, date, time, files, or pictures in the header. The dialog box has three sections: Left, Center, and Right for respective alignment of the header.
3 Place the insertion point as shown	Center section: **Outlander Spices** **Confidential**| You'll insert a picture in the center of the header.
Press (↵ ENTER)	To move to the next line. You'll insert the picture below the header text.

4 Click [image]	To open the Insert picture dialog box.
5 Navigate to the current unit folder	
Select **Logo**	You'll insert this picture in the header.
Click **Insert**	To return to the Header dialog box. The text "&[Picture]" appears in the Center section indicating that a picture will appear in the header.
6 Click **OK**	To return to the Page Setup dialog box, which displays a small preview of the new header.
Click **OK**	To close the Page Setup dialog box.
7 Choose **File, Print Preview**	To get a better idea of what the worksheet will look like when it's printed.
Click **Close**	To close the preview window.
8 Update the workbook	

Sending a range of cells via e-mail

Explanation

In Excel 2000, when you wanted to send Excel data to someone via e-mail, you had only two options: send an entire workbook or send an entire worksheet. With the new version of Excel, you can also send a selected range of cells. Here's how:

1 Select the range you want to send.
2 Choose File, Send To, Mail Recipient to open the E-mail dialog box.
3 Select Send the current sheet as the message body, and then click OK to activate Excel's integrated e-mail components. The file name is automatically entered in the Subject box.
4 In the To box, enter the recipient's e-mail address.
5 In the Introduction box, enter a message.
6 Click Send this Selection.

Do it!

A-5: Sending a range of cells via e-mail

Here's how	Here's why
1 Select A4:B16	
2 Choose **File**, **Send To**, **Mail Recipient**	To open the E-mail dialog box.
Select **Send the current sheet as the message body**	Though this option implies that the entire sheet will be sent, only the selected range will be included in the body of your message.
Click **OK**	To activate Excel's integrated e-mail components. These appear below the Formatting toolbar and above the worksheet.
3 In the To box, enter **ALS@OutlanderSpices.com**	
4 Edit the Subject box to read **First quarter sales**	
Click **Send this Selection**	To send only the selected cells to the recipient.
5 Start Outlook	Because Outlook is not configured to automatically send messages, the outgoing message is stored in your Outbox.
In the Folders List, click **Outbox**	
6 Open the message	Notice that only the selected range appears in the message body.
7 Close the message	
Close Outlook	
8 Deselect the cells	
Update the workbook	

Preventing single-column sorting

Explanation

A table contains related data arranged in rows across adjacent columns. When you sort only selected columns, the continuity across rows is broken and the data can become a confusing jumble of information. To prevent this problem, Excel 2002 automatically prompts you to expand your column selection to include all adjacent columns prior to sorting. Here's how it works:

1 Select the column by which you want to sort the table.

2 On the Standard toolbar, click the Sort Ascending button (or, if desired, the Sort Descending button). The Sort Warning dialog box will appear. By default, Expand the section is selected. By leaving this option selected, you ensure that the entire table will be sorted, thus preventing data continuity problems.

3 Click Sort to close the dialog box and sort the entire table by the originally selected column.

Do it!

A-6: Preventing single-column sorting

Here's how	Here's why
1 Select A5:A14	Notice that the product names appear in reverse alphabetical order.
2 Click [icon]	(The Sort Ascending button is on the Standard toolbar.) The Sort Warning message box appears stating that the columns next to the selected column would not be sorted. You can expand the selection to include all the columns or continue with the current selection.
3 Verify that Expand the selection is selected	To prevent single-column sorting. If this option is not selected, then data in only the selected columns will be sorted and the relation between the columns will be lost.
Click **Sort**	To sort the entire table based on the Product column. Notice that the product names now appear in alphabetical order and data continuity is maintained across each row.
4 Deselect the cells	
5 Update the workbook	

Topic B: Using smart tags in Excel

Explanation

Smart tags provide quick and easy access to frequently used options and commands. In this topic, you'll learn how to use Excel's Error Checking and the Stock Quote smart tags.

The Error Checking smart tag

Excel 2002 automatically reviews your formulas and notifies you of possible errors. If it finds a suspicious formula, a green triangle, or *smart tag*, will appear in the upper-left corner of the cell in which the formula is entered. When you select the cell, the Error Checking button appears. Pointing to the button displays a tool tip that describes the possible error. To address the problem, just click the button and choose the appropriate action from the shortcut menu.

Do it!

B-1: Using the Error Checking smart tag

Here's how	Here's why
1 Activate the West sheet tab	
2 Select F5	
3 Click ∑	
Select B5:D5	(Use your mouse.) To insert this range in the formula. Because you are not including the fourth quarter value in the formula, Excel will identify this formula as a possible error.
Press ⏎ ENTER	To enter the formula and calculate the value. Notice that a green triangle appears in the upper-left corner of the cell. This is the Error Checking smart tag.
4 Select F5	To display the Error Checking button.
5 Point to ◇	
	To activate the down arrow and display a tool tip that explains why Excel identified this formula as a possible error.

6 Click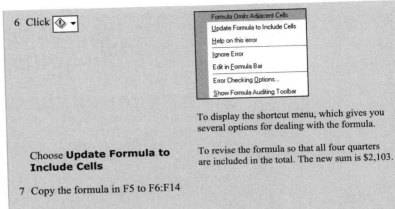

	Formula Omits Adjacent Cells
	Update Formula to Include Cells
	Help on this error
	Ignore Error
	Edit in Formula Bar
	Error Checking Options...
	Show Formula Auditing Toolbar

To display the shortcut menu, which gives you several options for dealing with the formula.

Choose **Update Formula to Include Cells**

To revise the formula so that all four quarters are included in the total. The new sum is $2,103.

7 Copy the formula in F5 to F6:F14

8 Deselect the range

9 Update the workbook

The Stock Quote smart tag

Explanation

By using the Stock Quote smart tag, you can insert and access Web-based financial information in a worksheet. To enable this feature, you must change one setting in the AutoCorrect dialog box, as follows:

1 Choose Tools, AutoCorrect Options to open the AutoCorrect dialog box.

2 Activate the Smart Tags tab.

3 Check Label data with smart tags.

4 Click OK.

After you make this setting, Excel will recognize stock symbols in your worksheets and flag them with the Stock Quote smart tag. You can then use the Smart Tags Actions menu to insert a refreshable stock price table in your workbook. You can also use the smart tag to start Internet Explorer and display stock quotes, business reports, and recent news about the selected company from the MSN MoneyCentral Web site.

Of course, to use any of these Stock Quote smart tag functions, you must have an active Internet connection.

Do it!

B-2: Using the Stock Quote smart tag

Here's how	Here's why
1 Choose **Tools, AutoCorrect Options...**	To open the AutoCorrect dialog box.
2 Activate the Smart Tags tab	
Check **Label data with smart tags**	To enable the Stock Quote smart tag.
Click **OK**	
3 In B20, enter **MSFT** and press ⏎ ENTER	This is the stock symbol for MSFT. Notice that a purple triangle appears in the lower-right corner of the cell. This is the Stock Quote smart tag.
4 Select B20	To activate the Smart Tag Actions button.
5 Click ⓘ ▾	To display the Smart Tag Actions menu.
6 From the list, select **Insert refreshable stock price**	To open the Insert Stock Price dialog box. By default, the stock quote table will be inserted on a new sheet. You also have the option of inserting it on the current sheet starting at a specific cell.
7 Click **OK**	To create a new worksheet and insert a stock quote table for Microsoft Corporation. The values in the table were downloaded from the Web and will be refreshed automatically while the workbook is open. The blue links are active and can be used to access additional financial information.
8 Activate the Report worksheet	
In B21, enter **DLM**	This is the stock symbol for Del Monte Foods.
9 Select B21	
Display the Smart Tag Actions menu	
Choose **Company report on MSN MoneyCentral**	To start Internet Explorer and display a company report for Del Monte Foods.
10 Close Internet Explorer	
11 Update the workbook	

Topic C: Using auditing features

Explanation

You can use the auditing features of Excel to track the value of a cell across worksheets and observe the calculations involved in a complex formula. You can do so by using the Watch Window and the Formula Evaluator respectively. Both of these can be accessed from the Formula Auditing toolbar. The toolbar also contains additional options to insert comments and trace errors.

The Watch Window

The Watch Window is used to keep track of a value in a particular cell (or cells). This is especially useful when you're changing values in one worksheet that are linked to values another worksheet. By using the Watch Window, you can see the effect of your changes immediately without switching between workbooks.

To track the value in a cell, right-click the cell and choose Add Watch from the shortcut menu to display the Watch Window (as displayed in Exhibit 1-1). This window, which will remain visible as you navigate in the workbook, displays six pieces of information about the selected cell, including the name of the workbook and worksheet in which it appears, its cell address, the current value, and its formula (if applicable). If the value in the cell changes, the new value will be reflected in the window immediately. When you no longer need to track the value, close the Watch Window.

Watch Window					▾ ✕
🖿 Add Watch... ✕ Delete Watch					
Book	Sheet	Name	Cell	Value	Formula
My yea...	Report		F16	$288,203	=SUM(B16:E16)

Exhibit 4-1: The Watch Window

Do it!

C-1:   Using the Watch Window

Here's how	Here's why
1 Right-click F16	(In the Report worksheet.) To display the shortcut menu.
Choose **Add Watch**	To open the Watch Window. It contains the name, address, value, and formula of the cell being watched. You can use this window to track the value in a particular cell within a worksheet as well as across worksheets.
2 Activate the South worksheet	Notice that the Watch Window remains visible. You'll change a linked value in this worksheet and observe the result in the Watch window.
3 Change the value in B8 to **$700**	This value is linked to the cell you're tracking in the Watch Window.
4 In the Watch Window, observe the Value column	The value has changed to reflect the updated sales figure. Because you used the Watch Window, you didn't have to switch to the Report sheet to observe this change.
5 Close the Watch Window	
6 Update the workbook	

The Evaluate Formula dialog box

Explanation

You can use the Evaluate Formula feature to calculate the different parts of a formula in sequence, one step at a time. This is especially useful when you need to "debug" a nested formula. By using the Evaluate Formula dialog box (as shown in Exhibit 4-2) you can calculate each component of a formula in the order that the formula evaluates them. By examining the results carefully, you can zero in on the specific part of the formula that might not be working the way you expected.

To use the Evaluate Formula feature:

1   Select the cell that contains the formula you want to evaluate.

2   Choose Tools, Formula Auditing, Evaluate Formula to open the Evaluate Formula dialog box. Under Evaluation, the formula is displayed with the first expression underlined.

3   Click Evaluate to calculate the underlined expression. The result is displayed in the formula and the next expression is underlined.

4   Click Evaluate to calculate the remaining expressions in sequence. You can also use the Step In button to display the formula represented by the underlined cell reference. To evaluate the reference and return to the previous reference, click Step Out.

5   When you're done, click Close to close the dialog box.

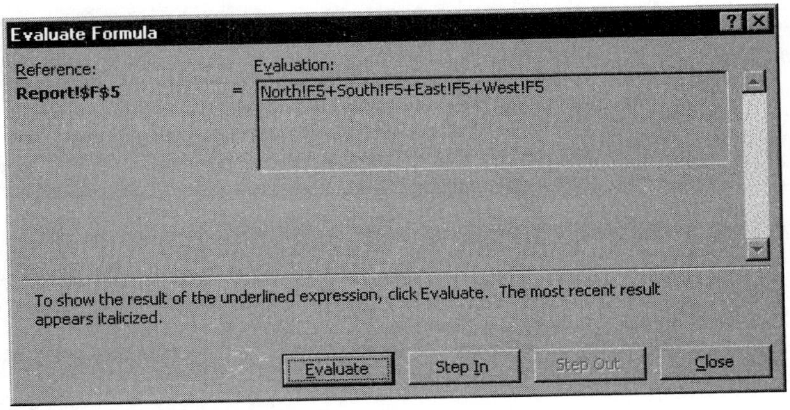

Exhibit 4-2: The Evaluate Formula dialog box

Do it!

C-2: Using the Formula Evaluator

Here's how	Here's why
1 Activate the Report worksheet	
2 Select F5	The formula in this cell calculates the total sales of anise seeds for the years 2001–2002. Looking at the formula bar, you can see that the calculated value is based on linked values in the four regional worksheets (North, South, East, and West).
3 Choose **Tools, Formula Auditing, Evaluate Formula**	To open the Evaluate Formula dialog box. Under Evaluation, the formula is displayed and the first expression (North!F5) is underlined.
Observe the dialog box	Note that the Evaluation box contains the formula of the selected cell and North!F5 is the underlined expression, as shown in Exhibit 4-2. You use the Evaluate button to view the result of the underlined expression in the formula. The Step In button is used to observe the steps involved in calculating a value and the Step Out button is used to go back to the previous step and formula.

4 Click **Step In**	Reference: Report!\$F\$5 = North!F5+South └ North!\$F\$5 = SUM(B5:E5)
	To display the formula represented by the underlined cell reference. The formula— SUM(B5:E5)—appears in the second box under Evaluation. Notice that the cell reference appears in blue.
5 Click **Evaluate**	Reference: Report!\$F\$5 = North!F5+South!F5+ └ North!\$F\$5 = \$2,103
	To calculate the formula in the second box. The value (\$2,103) appears in italics to indicate that it's the most recently calculated value.
6 Click **Step Out**	To insert the calculated value in the original formula. Notice that the next expression (South!F5) is underlined.
7 Calculate the value for the underlined expression	(Click Evaluate.) Again, the calculated value (3829) is inserted in italics. However, notice that instead of underlining the next expression, Excel underlines the first two values (2103+3829). This reflects the actual sequence in which the formula is calculated.
Click **Evaluate**	To sum the two underlined values. Notice that this time the next expression (East!F5) is underlined.
8 Evaluate the rest of the formula	Click Evaluate repeatedly until a single value (\$9,788) is displayed.
9 Click **Close**	To close the Evaluate Formula dialog box.
10 Update and close the workbook	

Unit summary: What's new in Excel 2002

Topic A In this unit, you learned how to **add colors to worksheet tabs**. Next, you learned how to draw custom borders by using the **border drawing tool** and use the **AutoSum list** to insert functions. You also learned how to **insert pictures in headers**, **mail only a range of cells**, and prevent **single-column sorting**.

Topic B Next, you learned how to use the **Error Checking smart tag** to detect and correct an error in a formula. You also learned how to use the **Stock Quote smart tag** to access and insert Web-based financial information.

Topic C Finally, you learned about two new auditing features. You used the **Evaluate Formula dialog box** to calculate a formula in sequence, one expression at a time. You also learned to evaluate a formula by using the **Formula Evaluator**.

Independent practice activity

1 Open Regional sales.

2 Apply a green color to the worksheet tab (any shade will do).

3 Use the border drawing tool to apply a blue, double-line border around the Total sales column.

4 Close the Borders toolbar.

5 Using the AutoSum list, calculate the average total sales for each region. (*Hint*: Enter the appropriate formulas in column E next to the respective regional subtotals.)

6 Insert Logo.gif in the worksheet's footer. Position the picture in the center section. (*Hint*: In the Page Setup dialog box, on the Header/Footer tab, click Custom Footer.)

7 Use Print Preview to verify that you inserted the picture in the footer correctly. When you're done, close the preview window.

8 Send only the East regional data via e-mail to **AFS@OutlanderSpices.com**

9 On a new sheet, insert a refreshable stock quote table for Dell Computer Corporation (stock symbol DELL). To do this, you'll need to use the Stock Quote smart tag.

10 Use the Watch Window to track the value in cell D47.

11 Save the workbook as **My regional sales**.

12 Close Excel.

Unit 5

What's new in PowerPoint 2002

Unit time: 45 minutes

Complete this unit, and you'll know how to:

A Use thumbnails in Normal view.

B Format presentations by using the Slide Design, Animation Schemes, and Custom Animation task panes.

C Use the Automatic Layout Options and AutoFit Options smart tags.

D Create a photo album, compress pictures, and save drawing objects and diagrams as pictures.

Topic A: **Working with thumbnails**

Explanation

In previous versions of PowerPoint, thumbnail navigation was available in only Slide Sorter view. Now, in PowerPoint 2002, you can use thumbnails in Normal view.

Thumbnail basics

In PowerPoint, *thumbnails* are miniature versions of each slide in your presentation. When you work in Normal view, you can use these thumbnails to navigate between slides. To do so, you must first activate the Slides tab on the left side of the application window.

Do it!

A-1: **Navigating with thumbnails in Normal view**

Here's how	Here's why
1 Start PowerPoint	
2 Open Performance speech	(From the current unit folder.) You'll navigate through the presentation by using the thumbnails.
3 Click as shown	
	(In the left pane.) To activate the Slides tab, which contains thumbnails of all the slides in the presentation.
4 Point to the third thumbnail	
	To display a tool tip indicating the slide's title.
5 Click the thumbnail	To display the third slide in the main area of the application window.
6 Navigate to the seventh slide	Scroll down in the Slides tab and click thumbnail #7.
7 Save the presentation as **My performance speech**	

Topic B: Using task panes in PowerPoint

Explanation

In PowerPoint 2002, you can apply slide designs and animation schemes by using task panes. You can also use a task pane to create custom animations.

Applying design templates

PowerPoint's built-in design templates make it easy to give a professional look and feel to your presentations. The design template you select usually depends on the presentation's purpose and target audience. You can apply a design template to a single slide, selected slides, or an entire presentation. When you apply a design template, PowerPoint automatically updates the text styles, graphics, and color scheme.

To apply a design template:

1 Select the slide(s) to which you want to apply the template. If you want to apply the template to the entire presentation, select any slide.
2 On the Formatting toolbar, click the Design button to display the Slide Design task pane.
3 In the task pane, point to the desired design template to activate the drop-down arrow.
4 Click the drop-down arrow to display the shortcut menu.
5 Choose the appropriate option: Apply to Selected Slides or Apply to All Slides.

Do it!

B-1: Using the Slide Design task pane

Here's how	Here's why
1 Click **Design**	(The Slide Design button is on the Formatting toolbar.) To display the Slide Design task pane, which actually consists of three different panes: Design Templates, Color Schemes, and Animation Schemes. By default, Design Templates is activated.
2 Under Available For Use, click as shown	To display the shortcut menu, which you can use to apply this design template to the selected slide or to the entire presentation.
3 Choose **Apply to Selected Slides**	To apply the Capsules template to only the selected slide. This change is reflected in both the main window and the thumbnail. Notice that the applied template now appears under Used in This Presentation (in the task pane).

<table>
<tr><td>

4 Under Apply a design template,
   click as shown

</td><td>

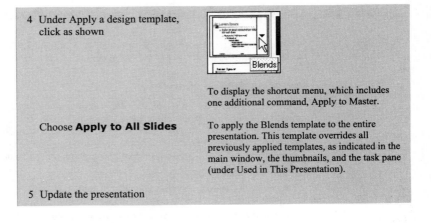

</td></tr>
<tr><td></td><td>

To display the shortcut menu, which includes
one additional command, Apply to Master.

</td></tr>
<tr><td>

Choose **Apply to All Slides**

</td><td>

To apply the Blends template to the entire
presentation. This template overrides all
previously applied templates, as indicated in the
main window, the thumbnails, and the task pane
(under Used in This Presentation).

</td></tr>
<tr><td>

5 Update the presentation

</td><td></td></tr>
</table>

Applying animation schemes

Explanation   You can also use the Slide Design task pane to apply PowerPoint's built-in animation
schemes. Here's how.

1 Select the slide to which you want to apply an animation scheme. If you want to
   apply the same animation scheme to all slides, select any slide.

2 If necessary, display the Slide Design task pane.

3 At the top of the task pane, click Animation Schemes to display a list of
   available schemes. (If the task pane is closed, you can go directly to this list by
   choosing Slide Show, Animation Schemes.) The list is divided into three
   sections: Subtle, Moderate, and Exciting.

4 From the Apply to selected slides list, select the desired scheme to apply it to the
   current slide. A preview of the animation will run once; to run the preview
   again, click Play. To apply the scheme to the entire presentation, click Apply to
   All Slides.

Do it!

B-2:   **Using the Animation Schemes task pane**

Here's how	Here's why
1 In the Slide Design task pane, click **Animation Schemes**	To display a list of PowerPoint's built-in animation schemes. This list is divided into three sections: Subtle, Moderate, and Exciting.
2 Select the first slide	Click the thumbnail in the Slides tab.
3 From the list of animation schemes, select **Pinwheel**	**Exciting** Big title Bounce Credits Ellipse motion Float Neutron Pinwheel Title arc (You'll find Pinwheel in the Exciting section.) To apply this scheme to the selected slide. In the main window, notice that a preview of the animation runs once.
4 Click **Play**	(At the bottom of the task pane.) To run the animation preview again.
5 Apply the **Dissolve in** scheme to the second slide	Select the second slide, and then select Dissolve in from the list of animation schemes (in the Subtle section).
6 Click **Slide Show**	(In the task pane.) To switch to Slide Show view.
7 Run the slide show	To observe the animation scheme that you applied to the second slide. Notice that you have to click the mouse (or press the down or right arrow key) to display each item on the slide.
End the slide show	Press the Esc key.
8 Update the presentation	

Customized animation schemes

Explanation

The Custom Animation task pane is used to add entry or exit animations, control timing, and synchronize all the effects in a presentation. You can add animation effects to a single object or to multiple objects. For example, you can animate bullet text to appear one letter at a time, one word at a time, or one paragraph at a time. When you animate an object it's indicated on the task pane as an animation event and on the slide by an animation tag, as shown in Exhibit 5-1. These are non-printing tags that are invisible when you run or print the presentation.

You can also specify the order and timing of your animations. For example, you can set them to occur automatically or only after you click the mouse. You can also preview the animation of your text and other objects to see how they'll work together.

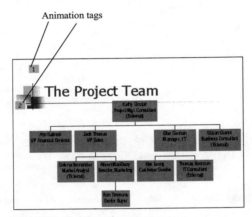

Exhibit 5-1: A slide with animation tags

Do it!

B-3:   Using the Custom Animation task pane

Here's how	**Here's why**
1 Select the last slide	You'll add custom animations to this slide.
2 Choose **Slide Show**, **Custom Animation...**	The Custom Animation task pane appears containing the Add Effect button to add effects to the selected section of the slide, and the Property and Speed lists to set the properties and speed of the animation, respectively. Note that all the options are disabled as nothing is selected on the slide.
3 In the current slide, select **The Project Team**	The Add Effect button is now available in the Custom Animation task pane.
4 Click **Add Effect**	

(At the top of the task pane.) To display the Add Effect menu.

Choose **Entrance**, **Fly In**	To apply a fly-in effect to the slide's title. On the slide, the applied effect is represented by the number 1 in a gray box next to the title.
5 Observe the task pane	

Notice that the drop-down lists become activated and the applied effect appears in the list area. You can use these lists to modify the applied effect. Also notice that the effect is marked with a mouse icon, which indicates that the animation will not run until you click the mouse.

6 From the Direction list, select **From Right**	To make the title fly in from the right side of the screen. A preview of the new setting is shown in the main window.
7 Select the organization chart starting with slide one	

8 Display the Add Effect menu	Click the Add Effect button in the task pane.
Choose **Entrance**, **Checkerboard**	To apply a checkerboard effect to the organization chart. Notice that a gray box with the number 2 appears next to the chart, indicating that the applied effect is second in the animation sequence. The effect is also added to the list in the task pane.
9 Click **Slide Show**	(In the task pane.) To run the presentation starting from the current slide. Notice that neither the title nor the chart appear automatically.
10 Click the mouse	To display the slide's title, which flies in from the right.
Click the mouse again	To display the organization chart, which appears with a checkerboard effect.
Press (ESC)	To end the slide show. Next, you'll modify the checkerboard effect so that the organization chart appears at the same time as the title.
11 Click as shown	![2 Object 2 drop-down]
	To display the drop-down list for the second object (the organization chart).
Select **Start With Previous**	So that the second animation will run simultaneously with the first animation.
12 From the Speed list, select **Slow**	To slow down the rate at which the organization chart will appear. Notice that a preview of the new setting is shown in the main window.
13 Switch to Slide Show view	(In the task pane, click Slide Show.) Again, neither the title nor the chart appears automatically.
Click the mouse	To start both animations simultaneously. Notice how slowly the chart fades in.
End the slide show	Press the Esc key.
14 Close the task pane	
Deselect the organization chart	
15 Update the presentation	

Topic C: Using smart tags in PowerPoint

Explanation

Like the other Office XP programs, PowerPoint 2002 features smart tags that provide convenient access to commonly used commands. In this topic, you'll learn about the Automatic Layout Options and AutoFit Options smart tags.

The Automatic Layout Options button

When you insert an object in a slide that already contains other items (text, graphics, and so on) PowerPoint automatically adjusts the slide layout to distribute the content as evenly and logically as possible. In some cases, however, you might want to override this automatic layout function so you can manually arrange the slide. To do so, you use the Automatic Layout Options button, which automatically appears when you insert an object. Just click the button to display the shortcut menu, and then choose Undo Automatic Layout. You can also use this menu to turn off the automatic layout function altogether.

Do it!

C-1: Using the Automatic Layout Options button

Here's how	Here's why
1 Move to the fifth slide	You'll insert a picture in this slide.
2 Click 🖼	(The Insert Picture button is on the Drawing toolbar.) To open the Insert Picture dialog box.
3 Navigate to the current unit folder	
4 Insert **Celebration**	(Select Celebration and click Insert.) Notice that the bullet text layout is automatically adjusted to accommodate the picture, which appears in the lower-right section of the slide. PowerPoint has anticipated the most logical placement of the picture and modified the slide layout accordingly.
5 Point to 🔁	(The Automatic Layout Options button is attached to the lower-right corner of the picture.) To activate the drop-down arrow.
6 Click 🔁 ▾	To display the shortcut menu, which you can use to override the automatic layout for only this picture or for all inserted objects.
Choose **Undo Automatic Layout**	To override the automatic layout. Notice that the picture is placed in the center of the slide, and the bulleted list returns to its original layout.

7 Display the Automatic Layout Options menu	Click the Automatic Layout Options button.
Choose **Redo Automatic Layout**	
Deselect the inserted picture	
8 Update the presentation	

The AutoFit Options button

When you add text to a slide, PowerPoint automatically adjusts the text to fit within the selected placeholder. To override this automatic formatting, you can use the AutoFit Options button. Just click the button to display the shortcut menu, and then choose Stop Fitting Text to This Placeholder.

Do it!
C-2: Using the AutoFit Options button

Here's how	Here's why
1 Place the insertion point as shown	• Free lunch every Wednesday • Free parking for one month| You'll add another item to this bulleted list.
2 Press (↵ ENTER)	
3 Type **Monthly surprise gifts**	As you type, notice that PowerPoint automatically resizes the list to fit in the placeholder. Also, the AutoFit Options button appears to the left of the placeholder.
4 Point to ⬌	To activate the drop-down arrow.
5 Click ⬌ ▾	To display the shortcut menu
Choose **Stop Fitting Text to This Placeholder**	To override the automatic resizing. Notice that the text now extends beyond the placeholder boundary.
6 Display the AutoFit Options menu	Click the AutoFit Options button.
Choose **AutoFit Text to Placeholder**	So that the list fits within the placeholder boundary.
7 Deselect the placeholder	
8 Update the presentation	

Topic D: **Working with pictures**

Explanation

In PowerPoint 2002, you can create a photo album of favorite pictures, compress pictures, and also save a slide as a picture.

Photo albums

In PowerPoint, a photo album is a presentation composed entirely of pictures. Before you create a photo album, it's a good idea to put all of the pictures you want to include in the same folder. Once you have done so, here's how you create the album:

1 Choose Insert, Picture, New Photo Album to open the Photo Album dialog box.
2 Under Insert picture from, click File/Disk to open the Insert New Pictures dialog box.
3 Navigate to the folder in which your pictures are stored.
4 Select the pictures you want to include in your album, and then click Insert to return to the Photo Album dialog box.
5 Under Album Layout, from the Picture layout list, select the desired layout.
6 If necessary, from the Frame shape list, select the desired shape.
7 If necessary, check Captions below ALL pictures. With this setting, each picture will be labeled with its file name.
8 Click Create to create a new presentation containing the selected pictures.

Do it!

D-1:   **Creating a photo album**

Here's how	Here's why
1 Choose **Insert**, **Picture**, **New Photo Album...**	To open the Photo Album dialog box.
2 Under Insert picture from, click **File/Disk**	To open the Insert New Pictures dialog box.
3 Navigate to the current unit folder	(If necessary.) You'll use these images to create a photo album.
4 Select all the pictures in the folder	Select any picture, and then press Ctrl+A.
Click **Insert**	To return to the Photo Album dialog box. Notice that all of the pictures have been added to the Pictures in album list, and a preview of the selected picture is displayed.
5 From the Pictures in album list, select **Celebration.gif**	You'll prevent this picture from being included in the album.
Click **Remove**	To delete it from the list.

6 Under Album layout, from the Picture layout list, select **1 picture**	You'll create a photo album with one picture on each slide, as shown in the preview.
7 From the Frame shape list, select **Corner Tabs**	So that each picture will have corner tabs, as shown in the preview.
8 Under Picture Options, check **Captions below ALL pictures**	With this setting, each picture will be labeled with its file name.
9 Click **Create**	To create a new presentation containing the selected pictures. By default, a title slide is inserted at the beginning of the presentation.
10 Run the slide show	Notice that the pictures are displayed one-to-a-slide and corner tabs appear around each picture. Also, the file names appear as captions under the pictures.
11 Save the presentation as **My photo album**	

Compressing pictures

Explanation

In some situations, you might find that the file size of your pictures is too large. For example, if you plan to publish a presentation on the Web, it's a good idea to make sure that each picture is small enough to download quickly. At the same time, however, you don't want to sacrifice image quality. To achieve both of these goals, you can use the Compress Pictures dialog box. Here's how it works.

1 In your presentation, select the picture you want to compress. If you want to compress all of the pictures in your presentation, select any picture.

2 If necessary, display the Picture toolbar.

3 On the Picture toolbar, click the Compress Pictures button to open the Compress Pictures dialog box.

4 Under Apply to, select the appropriate option: Selected pictures or All pictures in document.

5 Under Change resolution, select the appropriate option. Selecting Web/Screen will change the output resolution to 96 dots per inch (dpi); selecting Print will change the resolution to 200 dpi. You can also select No Change to maintain the current resolution.

6 Click OK.

Do it!

D-2: Compressing pictures

Here's how	Here's why
1 Activate the second slide	You'll compress the pictures in this presentation.
2 In the slide, select the picture	To display the Picture toolbar
3 Click [icon]	(The Compress Pictures button is on the Picture toolbar.) To open the Compress Pictures dialog box. Under Apply to, All pictures in document is selected by default.
4 Under Change resolution, select **Web/Screen**	With this setting, your pictures will be optimized for on-screen viewing—for example, via a Web browser. Each picture's resolution will be reduced to 96 dots per inch (dpi). Notice that you can also optimize your pictures for printing at a resolution of 200 dpi.
5 Click **OK**	The Compress Pictures message box appears stating that compressing pictures might reduce the quality of the pictures.
Click **Apply**	
6 Deselect the picture	
7 Update and close the presentation	

The Save as Picture dialog box

Explanation

When you create a drawing object or diagram in PowerPoint, you can save it as a separate picture file for use in other programs. To do so, you use the Save as Picture dialog box. Here's how:

1 Right-click the object to display the shortcut menu.
2 Choose Save as Picture to open the Save As Picture dialog box.
3 Navigate to the folder in which you want to save the file.
4 In the File name box, enter a file name.
5 From the Save as type list, select the desired format.
6 Click Save.

Do it!

D-3: Saving an object as a picture file

Here's how	Here's why
1 Activate the seventh slide	You'll save the organization chart as a picture.
2 Right-click the organization chart	To display the shortcut menu.
3 Choose **Save as Picture...**	To open the Save As Picture dialog box.
4 Navigate to the current unit folder	
5 Edit the File name box to read **Organization chart picture**	
6 From the Save as type list, select **GIF Graphics Interchange Format**	This browser-friendly file format is commonly used for pictures displayed on Web pages.
7 Click **Save**	To close the dialog box and save the picture file.
8 Update and close the presentation but don't close PowerPoint	

Unit summary: What's new in PowerPoint 2002

Topic A   In this unit, you learned that you can use **thumbnails in Normal view** to navigate through a presentation.

Topic B   Next, you learned how to format a presentation by using PowerPoint's **task panes**. Specifically, you used the **Slide Design** and **Custom Animation** task panes.

Topic C   Then, you learned how to use the **Automatic Layout Options** and the **AutoFit Options** smart tags.

Topic D   Finally, you learned how to create a **photo album, compress pictures**, and **save a drawing object or diagram as a picture**.

Independent practice activity

1   Open Presentation practice.

2   Open the Slide Design task pane.

3   Apply the **Crayons** design template to the entire presentation.

4   Open the Animation Schemes section of the Slide Design task pane.

5   Apply the **Compress** animation scheme to all of the slides in the presentation. (*Hint*: In the list of animation schemes, look under Moderate.) When you're done, run the slide show to verify that you've done this successfully.

6   Open the Custom Animation task pane.

7   Activate the fifth slide and select the table.

8   Apply the **Diamond** entrance to the table, and set it to start with the previous animation. Then, observe the slide in Slide Show view to confirm that you've done this correctly.

9   Activate the second slide.

10   Use the AutoFit Options button to split the bulleted list between slides 2 and 3. (*Hint*: To display the button, select the bulleted list placeholder.)

11   Compress all of the pictures in the presentation. Be sure to optimize them for viewing in a Web browser.

12   Save the presentation as **My presentation practice**.

13   Close PowerPoint.

Unit 6

What's new in Outlook 2002

Unit time: 40 minutes

Complete this unit, and you'll know how to:

A Use the AutoComplete Addressing feature, specify a different display name for a contact, work with active hyperlinks in the Subject box, and clean up your mailbox.

B Add color labels to appointments, edit Outlook's built-in labels, and apply color labels automatically.

Topic A: **Working with new e-mail features**

Explanation

Outlook 2002 provides several new and improved e-mail features, including:

- Expanded automatic completion of e-mail addresses
- The option of specifying a different display name for a contact
- Hyperlink support in the Subject box
- The Mailbox Cleanup dialog box

Automatic completion of e-mail addresses

In the previous version of Outlook, any contact name or e-mail address you entered in the To, Cc, or Bcc box would be completed automatically as you typed. In order for this to work, however, you must have already added the recipient to your Contacts folder. In Outlook 2002, automatic completion of e-mail addresses has been expanded to include any address to which you previously sent a message, regardless of whether the recipient is in your Contacts folder.

Do it!

A-1: Using AutoComplete addressing

Here's how	Here's why
1 Start Outlook	
2 Create a new e-mail message	(Click New on the Standard toolbar.) You'll create a draft message to be sent to Ann Salinski.
3 In the To box, enter **PMG@OutlanderSpices.com**	
	Note that the recipient is not in your Contacts folder, and this is the first time you're sending a message to this e-mail address.
In the Subject box, enter **Info request**	
In the body of the message, type **Please send current price list.**	
Send the message	Click the Send button on the Standard toolbar.
4 Create a new e-mail message	You'll enter the same recipient in the To box by using Outlook's expanded automatic completion feature.

5 In the To box, type **pmg**	Outlook completes the e-mail address automatically even though this recipient is not in your Contacts folder.
Press **Enter**	Notice that the e-mail address becomes underlined.
6 Save the message to your Drafts folder	Click the Save button on the Standard toolbar.

The Display as box

Explanation

In previous versions of Outlook, when you entered a contact in the To box, the recipient's complete e-mail was displayed automatically. In Outlook 2002, you can specify exactly how you want the contact's name to appear by using the Display as box in the Contact window.

Do it!

A-2:   Using the Display as box

Here's how	Here's why
1 In the To box, right-click **PMG@OutlanderSpices.com**	
	To display the shortcut menu. You'll add this recipient to your Contacts folder with a customized display name.
2 Choose **Add to Contacts**	To open the Contact window. Notice that the recipient's user name (PMG) is automatically entered in the Full Name box.
3 Edit the Full Name box to read **Paul M. Green**	
Observe the E-mail box	Paul's complete e-mail address is entered automatically.
4 Edit the Display as box to read **Paul**	So that only Paul's first name will appear in the To line when you send him an e-mail message.
5 Click **Save and Close**	To save and close your new contact and return to the message window.
6 Delete the contents of the To box	

7 In the To box, type **paul m. green**	To... paul m. green
Press **Tab**	To enter the contact name in the To box and move the insertion point to the Cc box. Notice that Paul's full name is automatically changed to just his first name. Also, his first name is capitalized because that's how you entered it in the Display as box.
8 Update the message	Click the Save button on the Standard toolbar.

Hyperlinks in the Subject box

Explanation For the first time, any hyperlink you enter in the Subject box will be an active, clickable link for both the sender and the recipient. In addition to entering Web URLs, you can use the following links to provide convenient access to other areas within Outlook:

Enter this...	To create a hyperlink to...
Inbox	Your Inbox
Contacts	Your Contacts folder
Mailbox folder	A specific mail folder
Calendar	Your Calendar
Message	A specific message in your inbox

Do it!

A-3: Using hyperlinks in the Subject box

Here's how	Here's why
1　In the Subject box, enter **Outlook:Calendar**	As you type, the text is converted to a blue, underlined hyperlink. You can use this hyperlink to open your Calendar.
2　Point to the hyperlink	The shape of the pointer changes to a hand.
3　Click the hyperlink	To open your Calendar to today's date.
4　Maximize the Calendar window	If necessary.
5　Click **New**	(The New Appointment button is on the Standard toolbar.) To start creating a new appointment.
6　In the Subject box, enter **Meeting with Jack**	
7　In the Location box, enter **Conference room**	
8　Schedule the appointment for tomorrow between 9:00 and 9:30 AM	Use the Start time and End time lists.
9　Click **Save and Close**	To save the appointment and return to the Calendar window.
10　Close the Calendar window	To return to the e-mail message.
11　In the body of the message, type **We have a meeting with Jack at 9:00 AM tomorrow in the conference room.**	
12　Click **Send**	To send the message.

Cleaning up your mailbox

Explanation

If your mailbox becomes overloaded with messages, you might experience slower overall performance in Outlook. To address this problem, you can use the Mailbox Cleanup dialog box (as shown in Exhibit 1-1) to:

- View the total size of your mailbox
- View the size of each folder in your mailbox
- Locate and delete items older than a specified date
- Locate and delete items larger than a specified KB size
- Using the AutoArchive feature to back up and then delete older messages
- Empty your Deleted Items folder with a single click

To open the Mailbox Cleanup dialog box, choose Tools, Mailbox Cleanup.

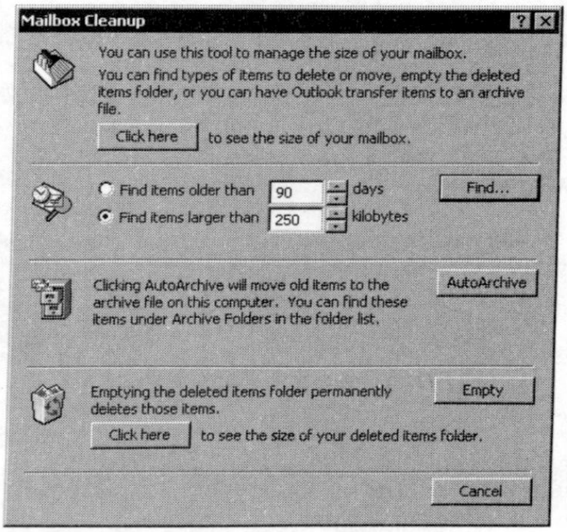

Exhibit 6-1: The Mailbox Cleanup dialog box

Do it!

A-4: Cleaning up the mailbox

Here's how	Here's why
1 Choose **Tools, Mailbox Cleanup...**	To open the Mailbox Cleanup dialog box.
2 At the top of the dialog box, click **Click here**	Click here · · · to see the size of your mailbox.
	To open the Folder Size dialog box, which displays the overall size of your mailbox as well as the size of each subfolder.
3 Click **Close**	To close the Folder Size dialog box.
4 Verify that Find items larger than, is selected	
In the kilobytes box, enter **20**	You'll find all mail items larger than 20 kilobytes (KB).
Click **Find**	To open the Advanced Find dialog box. At the bottom of the dialog box you'll see a list of mail items larger than 20 KB.
5 Right-click any message	To display the shortcut menu.
Choose **Delete**	To move the selected message to your Deleted Items folder.
Close the Advanced Find dialog box	
6 Open the Mailbox Cleanup dialog box	Choose Tools, Mailbox Cleanup.
7 Click **Empty**	A message box prompts you to confirm that you really want to permanently delete the entire contents of your Deleted Items folder.
Click **Yes**	To empty your Deleted Items folder.

Topic B: Calendar coloring

Explanation

In Outlook 2002, you can apply color labels to your appointments to indicate their respective priority levels and other significant information, such as whether an appointment is personal or business-related. Outlook's built-in labels can be modified to suit your work setting and individual style.

You can also automatically apply color labels based on specified conditions. For example, all appointments whose subject lines include the word "Sales" can be labeled with a particular color.

Color label basics

Just as you would use a pen to highlight important meetings in a day planner, you can apply color labels to the appointments in your Outlook Calendar. There are 10 different color labels, each of which has a different meaning. For example, the yellow label means that a meeting will be conducted over the phone.

To apply a color label to an existing appointment, right-click the appointment (to display the shortcut menu) and choose Label. Then, choose the desired label from the submenu. You can also apply a color label in the Appointment window by selecting the desired label from the Label list.

Do it!

B-1: Adding color labels to an appointment

Here's how	Here's why
1 Open your Calendar	Under Outlook Shortcuts, click the Calendar icon.
2 Display your appointments for tomorrow	(In the Date navigator, click tomorrow's date.) You have a meeting with Jack tomorrow morning at 9:00.
3 Right-click the appointment	To display the shortcut menu.

Choose **Label**

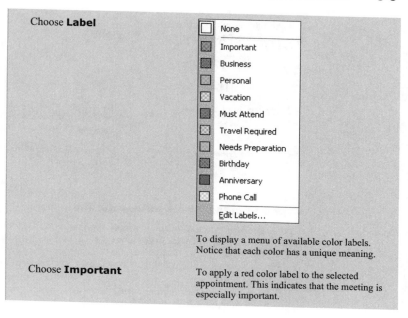

To display a menu of available color labels.
Notice that each color has a unique meaning.

Choose **Important**

To apply a red color label to the selected
appointment. This indicates that the meeting is
especially important.

Editing calendar labels

Explanation

If the built-in label definitions do not suit your work setting or personal style, you can
change them. Here's how:

1   On the Standard toolbar, click the Calendar Coloring button to display the
    Calendar Coloring menu.
2   Choose Edit Labels to open the Edit Calendar Labels dialog box.
3   Edit the text boxes to assign new meanings to the desired color labels.
4   Click OK.

Do it!

B-2:   Editing calendar labels

Here's how	Here's why
1 Click 🗒	(The Calendar Coloring button is on the Standard toolbar.) To display the Calendar Coloring menu.
2 Choose **Edit Labels**	To open the Edit Calendar Labels dialog box, which you can use to assign a different meaning to each color label.
3 Edit the first box to read **Sales Dept. Business**	From now on, the red label will denote appointments that are related to sales department business.

4 Edit the second box to read **Product Development**	
5 Click **OK**	To close the Edit Calendar Labels dialog box.
6 Open the appointment	Double-click the appointment.
7 Observe the Label box	Even though this appointment was created before you edited the color labels, the new meaning is assigned.
8 Close the appointment	Because you didn't change anything, there's no need to save it.

Applying color labels automatically

Explanation   You can configure Outlook to automatically apply color labels to appointments whose subject lines contain particular words. For example, you can have Outlook apply the yellow Phone Call label to all appointments whose subject lines contain the word "call." To do so, you use the Automatic Formatting Dialog box (as shown in Exhibit 6-2). Here's how it works:

1 From the Calendar Coloring menu, choose Automatic Formatting to open the Automatic Formatting dialog box.
2 Click Add to create an untitled rule.
3 In the Name box, enter a name for your rule.
4 From the Label list, select the desired label.
5 Click Condition to open the Filter dialog box. By default, the Appointments and Meetings tab is activated.
6 In the Search for the word(s) box, enter the word or phrase upon which you want the rule to be based.
7 From the In list, select the desired search location(s). You can have Outlook search in only the subject field, in both the subject and notes fields, or in all frequently used text fields.
8 Click OK to close the Filter dialog box.
9 Click OK to close the Automatic Formatting dialog box.

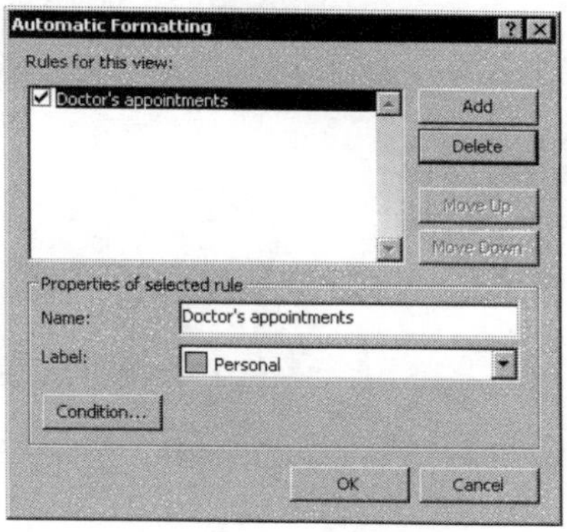

Exhibit 6-2: Auto Formatting dialog box

Do it!

B-3: Applying color labels automatically

Here's how	Here's why
1 Display the Calendar Coloring menu	Click the Calendar Coloring button on the Standard toolbar.
Choose **Automatic Formatting...**	To open the Automatic Formatting dialog box.
2 Click **Add**	To create an untitled entry under Rules for this view.
3 Edit the Name box to read **Doctor's appointments**	You'll create a rule so that all of your doctor's appointments are automatically labeled as personal time.
4 From the label list, select **Personal**	The green color label.
5 Click **Condition**	To open the Filter dialog box. By default, the Appointments and Meetings tab is activated.
In the Search for the word(s) box, enter **Dr.**	(Be sure to include the period.) With this setting, Outlook will automatically apply a green label to any appointment whose subject field includes the abbreviation "Dr." (for doctor).
Click **OK**	To close the Filter dialog box.

6 Click **OK**	To close the Automatic Formatting dialog box.
7 Create a new appointment	Choose File, New, Appointment.
8 In the Subject box, enter **Check-up with Dr. Garcia**	
Schedule the appointment for tomorrow between 3:00 and 4:00 PM	Use the Start time and End time lists.
Save and close the appointment	To return to the Calendar window.
9 Display your appointments for tomorrow	(If necessary.) Notice that a green color label is automatically applied to the new appointment.

Unit summary: What's new in Outlook 2002

Topic A

In this unit, you learned that Outlook 2002 will **automatically complete any e-mail address** to which you have previously sent at least one message. You also learned that you can specify exactly how a contact's name will appear in the To line of a message by using the **Display as box** in the Contact window. Then, you used the **Mailbox Cleanup** dialog box to optimize Outlook's performance.

Topic B

Next, you **applied color labels** to appointments in your Calendar. You also learned how to change the meaning of a color label. Finally, you configured Outlook to automatically apply a specific color label to any appointment whose subject line contained a particular word.

Independent practice activity

1 Create a new e-mail message and address it to **KTL@OutlanderSpices.com**.

2 In the Subject box, enter **http://office.microsoft.com**. Then, use the hyperlink to start Internet Explorer and go directly to Microsoft Office Tools on the Web. When you're done, close the browser to return to the message window.

3 In the To box, right-click the e-mail address to display the shortcut menu, and then choose **Add to Contacts**. Create a contact for **Kim Leong** so that when you send her a message, only her first name will appear in the To line. When you're done, save and close the contact to return to the message window.

4 To confirm that you completed step 3 correctly, delete the contents of the To box, enter **kim leong**, and press **Tab**. Outlook should automatically replace Kim's full name with just her first name.

5 In the message body, type **Click the URL to learn more about Office XP**, and then send the message.

6 Create a new appointment based on the following information:
   - Subject: Party for Natalie
   - Location: Conference room
   - Date: One week from today
   - Time: 4:00–5:00 PM

   When you're done, close the Appointment window.

7 Apply the **Birthday** color label to the new appointment.

8 Change the meaning of the gray color label from Vacation to **Optional**.

9 Configure Outlook to automatically apply a gray color label to any appointment whose subject field contains the word **optional**.

10 To confirm that you completed step 9 correctly, create a new appointment with the following subject: **Sales workshop (optional)**. You may specify any start and end time. When you close the Appointment window, the gray color label should be applied automatically.

11 Close Outlook.

Unit 7

Alternative user input

Unit time: 50 minutes

Complete this unit, and you'll know how to:

A Use speech recognition to control Office programs with your voice.

B Use the handwriting recognition feature.

C Use Office Document Imaging to send a scanned document to Word as editable text.

Topic A: Speech recognition

Explanation

You've probably seen science-fiction films or TV shows in which people use their voices to communicate with computers. This is no longer a futuristic vision. Thanks to Office XP's speech recognition feature, you can control Word, PowerPoint, Excel, Access, and Outlook by simply speaking into a microphone. You can do more than just dictate text into a document, however. You can also use your voice to access menu commands, select options, navigate through a file, "click" buttons, and so on. Keep in mind, however, that the extent to which you can control a program with your voice depends on which program you're working with.

Getting started with speech recognition

Before you start using speech recognition with Office XP, there are two operational factors to consider. First, the speech recognition feature is not designed for completely hands-free operation; you'll get the best results if you use a combination of your voice and the mouse or keyboard. Second, speech recognition works best in a quiet setting. If your work environment has a significant amount of background noise, then you might have some difficulty communicating with your computer through a microphone.

Microphones and other system requirements

Even if you work in a quiet office, you need to make sure that your computer is equipped with the proper hardware and software. First, you need a high quality close-talk microphone, also called a headset microphone. *Close-talk microphones* keep the microphone at a constant distance from your mouth. Once the microphone is positioned properly, the headset keeps it there no matter how you move your head.

Before you try to use the speech recognition feature, you should also make sure that your system has all of the following:

- 400 megahertz (MHz) or faster processor
- At least 128 MB RAM
- Windows 98 or later or Windows NT 4.0 or later
- Internet Explorer 5 or later

Activating speech recognition

To activate speech recognition in Word, PowerPoint, Access, or Outlook, choose Tools, Speech. In Excel, choose Tools, Speech, Speech Recognition.

Voice training

The first time you activate speech recognition, you'll be prompted to complete a process called voice training. During *voice training* the computer learns to recognize your voice by "listening" to you read a series of text passages displayed on the screen. As you speak, the voice training wizard indicates that it has "understood" you by highlighting each word in succession (as shown in Exhibit 7-1). This procedure, which takes about 15 minutes, also helps you to feel more comfortable with the headset, speak at the appropriate volume and speed, and position your microphone properly. The ideal microphone position is about an inch, or a thumb's width, to the side of your mouth. It should not be directly in front of your mouth, and you should avoid breathing directly into it.

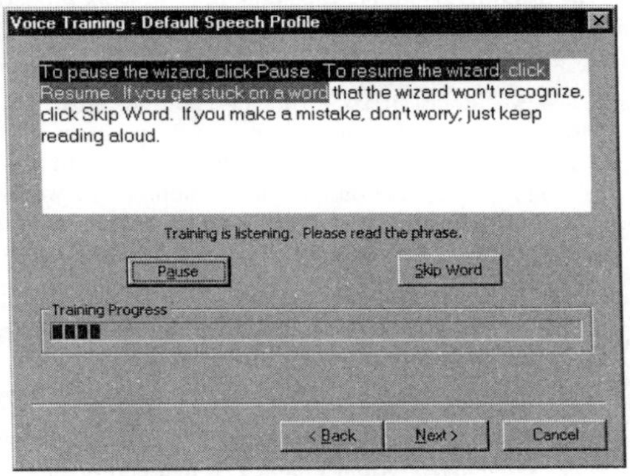

Exhibit 7-1: The Voice Training window

Introducing the Language bar

After you complete the initial voice training procedure, the Language bar (as shown in Exhibit 7-2) appears in the upper-right corner of the application window. This toolbar is your primary on-screen tool for working with speech recognition. It's a floating toolbar, so you can position it anywhere you want. You control the Language bar with your voice or by using your mouse.

Exhibit 7-2: The Language bar in voice command mode

To turn on speech recognition, click the Microphone button on the Language bar. The button will switch from gray to white to indicate that the computer is "listening." To turn off speech recognition, you can click the Microphone button again, or you can simply say "microphone."

When speech recognition is turned on, the Language bar also indicates which recognition mode is currently selected: dictation or voice command. You'll learn about these two modes in the following sections.

When you're not using speech recognition, you can close or minimize the Language bar. To close the bar, right-click it to display the shortcut menu, and then choose Close the Language bar. To redisplay the bar, choose Tools, Speech (in Excel, choose Tools, Speech, Speech Recognition).

To minimize the Language bar, click the minus sign (-) in the upper-right corner of the bar. When you do so, the Language bar icon (with the letters "EN," for English) appears on the taskbar next to the clock. To restore the Language bar, click the icon and then choose Show the Language bar.

Dictation mode

In *dictation mode*, the program listens to what you say, converts it to text, and enters that text at the insertion point. For dictation mode to work properly and consistently, thorough voice training is required. Otherwise, the program is likely to misinterpret what you say and enter the wrong text.

To activate dictation mode, click the Dictation button on the Language bar, or just say "dictation." As you speak, the program types. If the program still tries to interpret something you've said, it appears as a gray strip after the last typed word (as shown in Exhibit 7-3). To insert punctuation, just say the appropriate word—"period," "comma," and so on. It's possible, however, that the program will interpret these utterances as words to be typed. If so, you'll need to go back and make the necessary corrections.

Exhibit 7-3: The Language bar and sample text in dictation mode (from Word)

Voice command mode

In *voice command mode*, you use your voice to access menu commands, "click" buttons, select options, and so on. In this mode, you can do things with your voice that you would normally do with the mouse.

To activate voice command mode, click the Voice Command button on the Language bar, or say "voice command." From now on, the words you say will be interpreted as commands rather than dictated text, and each understood command will be displayed on the Language bar. For example, to display the File menu, say "file." You're not limited to the first-level menus, however. To go deeper into a menu, just say each word in succession. Thus, to open the Insert Table dialog box in Word, say "table, insert, table," pausing briefly between words. In the dialog box, you can use your voice to select options and "click" buttons by simply saying their names.

You can also use voice commands to navigate within a file. In Word, for example, you can say "home" to move the insertion point to the beginning of a line, or say "go end" to move it to the end of a line. To scroll down one page, say "page down;" to scroll up one page, say "page up."

For a complete listing of voice commands, consult the online Help system for the program you're working with.

Troubleshooting

If you experience problems while using the speech recognition feature, here are some things you can do:

- Conduct additional voice training—the more, the better. To do this, click the Tools button on the Language bar, and then choose Training.

- Check your microphone to make sure that it's working properly, and that it's in the correct position. You might even need to obtain a better quality microphone.

- Eliminate as much background noise as possible.

- Speak in a consistent, level tone. Speaking too loudly or too softly makes it difficult for the computer to recognize what you've said.

- When dictating text, speak without pausing between words; a phrase is easier for the computer to interpret than just one word. Also, pronounce words clearly, but don't separate or overemphasize each syllable in a word.

- If a voice command doesn't appear to work, switch to another program, switch back to the program you were working in, and then say the command again. If the command doesn't work as expected by the third or fourth try, don't continue to repeat the command. Instead, use your mouse or keyboard.

- For additional assistance, consult the online Help system.

Do it!

A-1: Discussing speech recognition

Question	Answer
1 What are the system requirements for speech recognition?	
2 What is the purpose of voice training?	
3 What are the two modes of speech recognition?	
4 What can you do if the speech recognition feature fails to accurately interpret what you say?	
5 How do you initiate additional voice training?	

Topic B: Handwriting recognition

Explanation

When your typing skills (or lack thereof) lead to frustration with the keyboard, you might want to try Office XP's handwriting recognition feature. Using your mouse or a special input device, you can write out your text longhand, and the current Office program will convert it into typed text. This feature is also useful for creating simulated signatures in Word or Outlook.

Getting started

If you want to use handwriting recognition, you don't need any special accessories. That is, you can use your mouse to simulate the act of writing by hand. However, you'll probably find it more comfortable to work with some sort of tablet device. Commonly used with graphics programs, a *tablet* system consists of a flat, electronically sensitive input surface and a pen-like stylus device. You use the stylus to write on the tablet the same way you would use a pencil to write on a sheet of paper. Before you install a tablet system for the purpose of handwriting recognition, you should make sure that it's compatible with Office XP.

Also, it's important to note that in order to use handwriting recognition in Outlook, you must use Word as your e-mail editor.

Activating handwriting recognition

After you install the handwriting recognition feature, the Language bar appears automatically when you start any Office program. You use the buttons on the Language bar to turn handwriting recognition on and off, modify your handwriting settings, make corrections, and switch between the Writing Pad and Write Anywhere mode (you'll learn about these tools later in this topic).

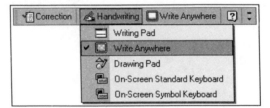

Exhibit 7-4: The Language bar with the Handwriting menu displayed

Text mode vs. ink mode

Before you start working with the Language bar and handwriting recognition, it's important to understand the difference between the two recognition modes: text mode and ink mode.

In *text mode*, whatever you write is converted into typed text and entered at the insertion point. This is the most common application of handwriting recognition.

In *ink mode*, which is available in only Word and Outlook, your handwriting is turned into graphics called *ink objects*. You can think of ink objects as small drawings that look exactly like your own handwriting. For this reason, ink mode is often used to create simulated signatures. Once inserted, you can format an ink object in many of the same ways that you would format typed text. For example, you can make an ink object bigger by applying a larger point size, or you can make it stand out on the page by applying bold formatting or a different color.

Finally, you can convert an ink object to typed text by right-clicking the object to display the shortcut menu, and then choosing Ink Object, Recognize.

The Writing Pad

The Writing Pad is a separate window in which you write the text to be inserted into your document. You activate the Writing Pad by clicking the Handwriting button on the Language bar (to display the Handwriting menu) and then choosing Writing Pad. You should position the Writing Pad so that it doesn't obscure your view of the text as it's inserted in the document.

When you point to the writing area, your mouse pointer changes to a pen (as shown in Exhibit 7-5). The horizontal line in the writing area can help you keep your writing straight and neat, thus making it easier for the program to correctly interpret the text. Outside of the writing area, your mouse functions normally.

Exhibit 7-5: The Writing Pad with sample text

On the right side of the Writing Pad you'll find a collection of buttons. The following table describes the function of each button.

Button	What it does
🖋	Activates ink mode (available only in Word and Outlook).
⊤	Activates text mode.
✎	Displays the drawing pad, which you can use in ink mode to create simple drawings (not available in Excel or Access).
⌨	Displays the on-screen standard keyboard, which you can use just like a regular keyboard, except you click the keys with your mouse.
←	Same as pressing the Backspace key.
↵	Same as pressing the Enter key.
Space	Same as pressing the spacebar.
Tab	Same as pressing the Tab key.
↑ ← → ↓	Moves the insertion point up, down, left, or right (same as pressing the arrow keys).
📝	If the program is not set up for automatic recognition, pressing this button triggers the program to convert what you've written in the writing area.
▣	Switches to Write Anywhere mode.
🗐	Selects the current item and displays a list of alternative spellings.
⌀	Clears the contents of the writing area.
≪ or ≫	Expands or reduces the number of buttons shown on the Writing Pad.

About automatic recognition

By default, your handwriting is converted automatically as you write. This automatic conversion occurs whenever you pause between words. Even if you leave spaces between words, the program will not convert the text until you actually stop writing for a moment. Any spaces you leave between words will be entered as space characters in the document.

In some situations you might want to turn off automatic recognition. To do so, you use the Handwriting Options dialog box (as shown in Exhibit 7-6). Here's how:

1   Click the down arrow in the upper-left corner of the Writing Pad to display the Writing Pad menu.

2   Choose Options to open the Handwriting Options dialog box. By default, the Common tab is activated.

3   Clear Automatic recognition.

4   Click OK.

By turning off automatic recognition, you give yourself a chance to examine what you've written before it's converted and entered in a document. This can be especially useful when you create a simulated signature in ink mode. If the signature doesn't look right to you, you can clear the writing area by clicking the Clear button. When your signature looks the way you want it to, click the Recognize Now button to enter the ink object in your document.

Exhibit 7-6: The Handwriting Options dialog box

Turning off handwriting recognition

When you want to stop using handwriting recognition, close the Writing Pad by clicking the Writing Pad button on the Language bar, or by clicking the Close button in the upper-right corner of the Writing Pad.

Do it!

B-1: Using the Writing Pad to insert an ink object

Here's how	Here's why
1 Start Word	
Open Memo 1	From the current unit folder.
Place the insertion point in the indicated position	Sincerely, | Jack Thomas, VP Sales
	You'll insert a simulated signature by using the Writing Pad.
2 Click **EN**	(On the task bar, next to the clock.) To display the shortcut menu.
Choose **Show the Language bar**	To display the Language bar, which appears at the top of the application window.
3 Click **Handwriting**	(On the Language bar.) To display the Handwriting menu.
Choose **Writing Pad**	
	To activate the Writing Pad. By default, the Text button is selected, indicating that text mode is activated. In this mode, whatever you write is converted into typed text and entered at the insertion point.
Click	To switch to ink mode, in which your handwriting is turned into graphics called ink objects. This mode can be used to create simulated signatures.
4 Click as shown	
	To display the Options menu for the Writing Pad.
Choose **Options**	To open the Handwriting Options dialog box. By default, the Common tab is activated. Under Recognition, notice that Automatic recognition is checked.

5   Clear **Automatic recognition**

By turning off automatic recognition, you give yourself a chance to examine what you've written before it's converted and entered in the document.

Click **OK**

To close the dialog box.

6   On the Writing Pad, in the writing area, write **Jack** as shown

(Drag the mouse.) When you stop writing, the word is not inserted in the document because you turned off automatic recognition.

Click [✎]

(The Clear button is on the right side of the Writing Pad.) To erase the contents of the writing area so you can try again.

7   On the Writing Pad, in the writing area, write **Jack** again

Click [▣]

(The Recognize Now button is on the right side of the Writing Pad.) To insert the signature as an ink object.

On the Language bar, click **Writing Pad**

To close the Writing Pad.

8   Select the ink object

(Use the mouse.) You can format ink objects in many of the same ways that you format typed text.

From the Font Size list, select **48**

To make the signature bigger.

Make the signature blue

(Any shade will do.) Use the Font Color palette on the Formatting toolbar.

9   Save the document as **My memo 1**

In the current unit folder.

Write Anywhere

Explanation

If you don't want to use the Writing Pad, you can work in Write Anywhere mode. To activate this mode, display the Handwriting menu (on the Language bar) and choose Write Anywhere. In this mode, you can literally write anywhere on the screen. The floating Write Anywhere toolbar provides the same buttons as the Writing Pad, and most of the procedures are the same. It's important to note, however, that in Write Anywhere mode you cannot use the mouse to select text in the document area, nor can you use it to drag the scrollbars.

Switching to the Writing Pad

To switch from Write Anywhere mode to the Writing Pad, click the Writing Pad button on the Write Anywhere toolbar, or choose Writing Pad from the Handwriting menu.

Turning off handwriting recognition

In Write Anywhere mode, when you want to stop using handwriting recognition, click the Write Anywhere button on the Language bar, or click the Close button in the upper-right corner of the Write Anywhere toolbar.

Do it!

B-2: Using Write Anywhere mode to insert typed text

Here's how	Here's why
1 Place the insertion point in the indicated position	Jack Thomas, VP Sales
2 Display the Handwriting menu	On the Language bar, click Handwriting.
Choose **Write Anywhere**	To display the Write Anywhere toolbar.
3 Switch to text mode	Click the Text button on the Write Anywhere toolbar.
4 Turn on automatic recognition	Click the down arrow in the upper-left corner of the Write Anywhere toolbar, choose Options, check Automatic recognition, and click OK.

5 Write **North** anywhere on the screen

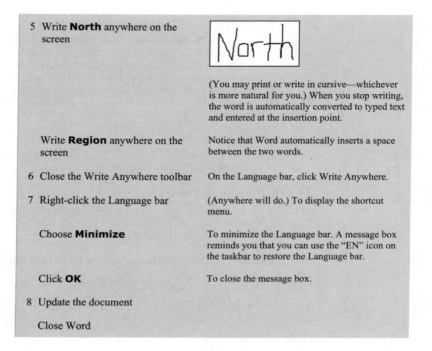

(You may print or write in cursive—whichever is more natural for you.) When you stop writing, the word is automatically converted to typed text and entered at the insertion point.

Write **Region** anywhere on the screen

Notice that Word automatically inserts a space between the two words.

6 Close the Write Anywhere toolbar

On the Language bar, click Write Anywhere.

7 Right-click the Language bar

(Anywhere will do.) To display the shortcut menu.

Choose **Minimize**

To minimize the Language bar. A message box reminds you that you can use the "EN" icon on the taskbar to restore the Language bar.

Click **OK**

To close the message box.

8 Update the document

Close Word

Topic C: Working with Office Document Imaging

Explanation   You receive a hard copy manuscript that you want to recreate in Word. If the original document is not available in electronic form, you can scan the pages and then use the Office Document Imaging program to send the scanned document to Word as typed text.

Most scanning programs give you the option of saving scan files in several different formats, such as bitmap (.bmp) or TIFF (.tif). TIFF, which stands for stands for *Tagged Image File Format*, is the only format supported by Office Document Imaging. Therefore, if you want to turn a scanned document into Word text, you must save the scan as a TIFF file. The imaging program can handle single- or multi-page TIFFs.

Getting started

To start the imaging program, choose Start, Programs, Microsoft Office Tools, Microsoft Office Document Imaging.

The next step is to open the TIFF file you want to translate. Here's how:

1   Click the Open button on the toolbar (or choose File, Open) to open the Open dialog box.
2   Navigate to the folder that contains the TIFF file.
3   Select the desired file.
4   Click Open.

At this point, the program window will look similar to Exhibit 7-7. If you're working with a multi-page TIFF, the first page will appear in the right pane, and a series of thumbnail (or miniature) images will appear in the left pane. You can navigate among the various pages by clicking the thumbnails (or by using the Page arrows on the toolbar). If you're working with a single-page TIFF, there will be only one thumbnail image.

To change the magnification in the right pane, you have three options:

- Choose View, Zoom to open the Zoom dialog box, and then drag the slider to zoom in or out.
- On the toolbar, select the desired magnification from the Zoom list.
- On the toolbar, click the Zoom In or Zoom Out button.

To view the document in full-screen mode, click the Reading View button on the toolbar, or choose View, Reading View. To get out of full-screen mode, press the Esc key.

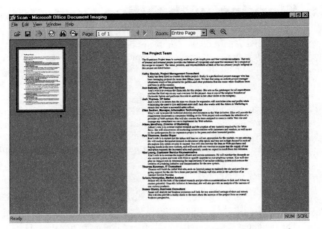

Exhibit 7-7: The Office Document Imaging window with a sample scan

Sending an entire document to Word

If you want to send all of the scanned text to Word, here's what you do:

1 On the toolbar, click the Send Text to Word button (or choose File, Send Text to Word). The first time you do this, a message box indicates that the program must first decipher the text through a process called *optical character recognition*, or *OCR*. To proceed, click OK.

2 After a moment, the Send Text to Word dialog box appears. Select All pages.

3 Click OK to create a new Word document that contains the converted text.

The Word document does not reflect the formatting of the original document, although paragraph and list structures might be maintained. In most cases, you need to manually format the text. You should also review the Word document carefully to ensure text accuracy.

Sending part of a document to Word

If you don't need to recreate the entire document, you can send a portion of the scanned text to Word. Here's how:

1 In the right pane, display the page that contains the text you want to send to Word.

2 Drag the mouse to draw a red box around the desired text.

3 Click the Send Text to Word button. (The first time you do this in the current TIFF file, the OCR message box appears. Click OK to proceed.)

4 After a moment, the Send Text to Word dialog box appears. By default, Current selection is selected. Click OK to create a new Word document containing the selected text.

Do it!

C-1: Converting a scanned image to editable text

Here's how	Here's why
1 Choose **Start, Programs, Microsoft Office Tools, Microsoft Office Document Imaging**	To start Microsoft Office Document Imaging.
Maximize the application window	If necessary.
2 Click 🗁	(On the toolbar.) To open the Open dialog box. You'll open a scan file and convert it to editable text.
3 Navigate to the current unit folder	
Select **Scan 1**	This is a single-page TIFF (.tif) file. TIFF is the only scan format supported by the imaging program.
Click **Open**	To display the selected scan file in the right pane of the application window. Notice that a thumbnail version appears in the left pane.
4 From the Zoom list, select **Page Width**	To view the page with its full width taking up the right pane.
5 Click ⌨	(On the toolbar.) To send the scan to Word. A message box indicates that the imaging program must first decipher the page via optical character recognition (OCR) before exporting the text.
Click **OK**	To proceed with the OCR process, as represented by the progress bar. When this process is completed, the Send Text to Word dialog box appears. By default, Selected pages is selected.
6 Select **All pages**	To export the entire document.
Click **OK**	To create a new Word document containing all of the scanned text.
7 Save the document as **Project team**	In the current unit folder.
Close Word	To return to the imaging program.
8 Choose **File, Exit**	To close the imaging program. When you're prompted to save changes, click No.

Unit summary: Alternative user input

Topic A   In this unit, you learned that you can use the **speech recognition** feature to control the various Office programs by using your voice. You learned the difference between **dictation mode** and **voice command mode**, and you learned that accurate speech recognition requires extensive **voice training**. You also learned how to work with the **Language bar**.

Topic B   Then, you learned how to use the **handwriting recognition** feature. You used the **Writing Pad** in **ink mode** to create a simulated signature. You also learned how to turn **automatic recognition** on and off. Then, you used **Write Anywhere mode** in combination with **text mode** to convert your handwriting to typed text.

Topic C   Finally, you used the **Office Document Imaging** program to export a scanned document to Word as editable text. You also learned that **TIFF** is the only scan format supported by the imaging program.

Independent practice activity

1   Start Excel and open Handwriting practice.

2   Activate the Language bar, and then display the Writing Pad.

3   Turn off automatic recognition. (*Hint*: Use the Handwriting Options dialog box.)

4   Use the Writing Pad in text mode to enter the following sales values for Anise Seeds.

- Qtr1: **$100**
- Qtr2: **$250**
- Qtr3: **$320**
- Qtr4: **$500**

5   Close the Writing Pad (but don't close the Language bar).

6   Save the workbook as **My handwriting practice**, and then close Excel.

7   Start Word and open Memo 2.

8   Use the Writing Pad in ink mode to insert a simulated signature for Kathy Sinclair. Make the ink object blue (any shade will do) and make sure that it's big enough to read clearly. When you're done, the signature should look as realistic as possible.

9   Close the Writing Pad, and then minimize the Language bar.

10   Save the document as **My memo 2**, and then close Word.

11   Start Microsoft Office Document Imaging and open Scan 2.

12   Display the entire page in the right pane.

13   Send only the last paragraph to Word as editable text. (*Hint*: Use your mouse to draw a box around the paragraph.)

14   Save the Word document as **My paragraph**, and then close Word.

15   Close Microsoft Office Document Imaging (do not save changes).

Office XP:
New Features
Quick reference

Button	Keystrokes	What it does
		Opens the Basic Search task pane
		Expands the toolbar to show more buttons
		Displays the AutoCorrect options menu
		Displays the Paste Options menu
		Opens the Diagram Gallery dialog box
		Displays the Clip Art task pane
		Displays the Style and Formatting task pane
		Italicizes the selected text
		Displays lines between rows and columns
		Opens the Insert Picture dialog box
		Sorts the data in ascending order
		Calculates the sum of a range of data
		Displays the Error Checking Options menu
		Displays or hides the Watch Window

Button	Keystrokes	What it does
		Opens the Evaluate Formula dialog box
		Displays the AutoFit Options menu
		Opens the Compress Pictures dialog box
		Displays the Calendar Coloring menu

Index